TWILIGHT
OF LOVE

The author's other works include:

The Mysterious Tales of Ivan Turgenev (trans.)
Turgenev: the Quest for Faith
Anthology of Australian Gay and Lesbian Writing (ed.)
A Mother's Disgrace
Night Letters
Secrets (with Drusilla Modjeska and Amanda Lohrey)
Speaking Their Minds: intellectuals and the public culture (ed.)
(and so forth)
Corfu

Robert Dessaix

TWILIGHT
OF LOVE

TRAVELS WITH TURGENEV

Scribner

First published in Australia by Pan Macmillan Australia Pty Ltd, 2004
First published in Great Britain by Scribner, 2005
An imprint of Simon & Schuster UK Ltd
A Viacom Company

1 3 5 7 9 10 8 6 4 2

Simon & Schuster UK Ltd
Africa House
64–78 Kingsway
London WC2B 6AH

www.simonsays.co.uk

Simon & Schuster Australia
Sydney

A CIP catalogue record for this book is available from the British Library

'A Prince from Western Libya' from *Collected Poems* by C.P. Cavafy translated by
Edmund Keeley and Philip Sherrard and published by Hogarth Press. Used by
permission of the Estate of C.P. Cavafy and The Random House Group Ltd.

If the author has inadvertently quoted from any text or verse in copyright, the
publisher will be pleased to credit the copyright holder in all future editions.

ISBN: 0-7432-6338-3
EAN: 9780743263382

Printed and bound in Great Britain by
Mackays of Chatham plc

For Natalie Staples

'Love is the final metaphor of sexuality. Its
cornerstone is freedom: the mystery of the person.'

OCTAVIO PAZ, *The Double Flame*

He wasn't a profound thinker or anything at all –
just a piddling, laughable man.
He assumed a Greek name, dressed like the Greeks,
learned to behave more or less like a Greek;
and all the time he was terrified he'd spoil
his reasonably good image
by coming out with barbaric howlers in Greek
and the Alexandrians, in their usual way,
would start to make fun of him, vile people that they are.

From 'A Prince from Western Libya', C.P. CAVAFY
(translated by Edmund Keeley and Philip Sherrard)

THE BACKGROUND

One Saturday morning when I was about eleven or twelve years old, at about the time the first sputnik began crisscrossing the sky, I went into my local bookshop in a suburb of Sydney and bought myself a Russian dictionary. Exactly why I chose a Russian dictionary instead of an Italian or Spanish one I no longer remember. I doubt that it was because of the sputnik we used to rush out into the street at night to see, although in the mid-1950s the Soviet Union did give the impression of being on a soaring trajectory in all sorts of exciting ways. What I do remember is hurrying home with my little dictionary to see if I could decode the enigmatic squiggles on the splendid Soviet stamps in my collection. To this day I vividly recall my sense of triumph when I finally worked out that the line of funny box-shaped letters on one of the stamps meant 'Botanical Gardens'.

Although I didn't know it at the time, in the blink of an eye that Saturday morning, when I reached up and pulled that book down from the bookshop shelf, the whole course of my life changed. 'Oh what a dear ravishing thing is the beginning of an Amour,' says one of the characters in Aphra Behn's comedy *The Emperor of the Moon*. Indeed it is and, despite my tender age, ravished is what I was, and Russian was my new-found Amour – not a wholly wise one, no doubt, from many people's point of view (it *was* the 1950s), although, strangely, nobody ever said anything to discourage it.

Within weeks I'd joined an evening class to pursue my new-found love. Then, still unsatisfied, I sought out a private tutor and, eventually, after a year studying at Moscow University, I began teaching Russian language and literature to students hardly younger than I was. Russia, and especially its marvellous language, became my life. Once or twice over the years I've regretted not going home with an Italian dictionary that morning, or even a Portuguese one, something that might have opened a window onto a sunnier, more approachable world than Russia proved to be. But not often. It's true that I've remained irre-deemably un-Russian – everything about me comes from somewhere else – but that may be the secret of my lifelong obsession with all things Russian: it's more a love-affair than a friendship, and to love like that with any lasting pleasure it's sometimes best to be aware of your fundamental unlikeness.

To my surprise, writing about Russia has proved extraordinarily difficult. Perhaps it's like writing about your spouse or your children: on the one hand, you have so many things to say you hardly know where to start; on the other hand, you simply feel no need to turn what is still kaleidoscoping before your eyes into words, into a mere story. Over the nearly forty years since I first arrived in Moscow as a student in 1966, Russia has changed beyond all imagining (and also, curiously, hardly at all), as I suppose I have myself, along with my fraught love for the country. Since that first stint at Moscow University I've visited Russia many times, as a student, as a tourist and also just to be there again, to walk the streets, smell the smells, eat the food and have long conversations with old friends who couldn't until recently even dream of visiting me. Yet to talk about the 'song resounding ceaselessly in my ears', as Nikolai Gogol puts it in *Dead Souls*, 'clutching at my heart' (it doesn't sound at all overblown when

Gogol says it, just poetic and heart-breakingly true), has seemed almost impossible.

Then in Baden-Baden, Germany, while I was zigzagging across Europe one summer, I chanced upon the traces of Turgenev. He lived there for seven years in the 1860s – indeed, is said to have ceased being a Russian there and become a German, despite being his country's most celebrated writer at the time. Although Ivan Sergeyevich Turgenev's novels and short stories had never been a passion of mine – his storylines were not strings of extravagant marvels, like Gogol's, he didn't thunder and rage like Dostoyevsky, he painted no panoramas on the scale of *War and Peace* – I had decades earlier spent some years reading almost every word he wrote, right down to his laundry lists, and I had spent most of my second stint at Moscow University in 1970 delving into every old journal and critical work I could lay my hands on to find out everything I could about him. Nothing he wrote had struck me like a bolt of lightning, nothing I'd read had changed night into day, but over time – over decades – I'd begun to feel for Turgenev what T.S. Eliot, reflecting on a writer's relationship to towering literary figures, has called 'a profound kinship, or rather . . . a peculiar personal intimacy' charged with 'secret knowledge'. You feel you've become the great writer's 'friend', he says, and that friendship, allowing you to 'penetrate at once the thick and dusty circumlocutions about his reputation', broadens and changes you as any true intimacy must. Intimate friendship always takes some time to flower (unlike love, which can be instantaneous) and in my case it took some thirty years.

First in Baden-Baden, later around Paris and finally in Russia, where he also spent large slices of his life, I found that following in Turgenev's footsteps, seeking not his ghost but to understand our kinship better, made me want to write. At one level I wanted to write about the various obsessions that we share, Ivan Sergeyevich and I, but mainly I wanted at long last to write about Russia – my Russia, not an economist's or political scientist's. And so crabwise, as it were, while seeming to fix my sights on Turgenev, I have ended up scuttling past him, heading for a broader target.

Turgenev lived, I think, in a twilight time between utterly different ways of construing the world – politically, religiously, philosophically. He himself swung like a pendulum between Romanticism on the one hand and something darker, more mercilessly reasoned and, of course, more recognisably modern on the other. It was in this twilit space between eras, as I see it, that love as it had been understood for centuries became difficult. Over a century later, I believe, this kind of love is almost impossible – not completely out of the question, but very nearly. In these encounters with Ivan Sergeyevich Turgenev, although it's by no means the only thing he speaks to me about, it's the way he illuminates this theme – how to love in love's twilight – that 'clutches at my heart'.

Robert Dessaix
Hobart, Tasmania
2003

NOTE

In English, French and German, Russian names are spelt in a bewildering variety of ways. The name of the author of *Fathers and Sons*, for example, pronounced in Russian something like *toor-GYE-nyef*, can turn up as Turgeniev, Tourguénev, Tourguénieff, Turgenjew and various combinations of all of those. My approach in this book has been to choose one common spelling of Russian names and stick to it. Hence:

Chekhov
Dostoyevsky
Oryol (rather than Orel)
Spasskoye
Tolstoy
Turgenev

The translations from Russian and French are my own. However, I admit that on occasion, particularly when translating dialogue, I have adopted an English version which particularly suits my own narrator's voice.

A brief chronology of Turgenev's life and works appears at the end of the book.

PART ONE

BADEN-BADEN

'His domestic circumstances . . . were not such as to attach him to his native land.'

VIRGINIA WOOLF, WRITING ABOUT TURGENEV IN
'A GIANT WITH VERY SMALL THUMBS'

'*MEINE DAMEN UND HERREN, in wenigen Minuten erreichen wir Baden-Baden.*' Gently braking. 'Ladies and gentlemen, next stop –'

BADEN-BADEN. Gliding into the station. BADEN-BADEN. Snack-bar. Lady with lapdog. Hardly a soul about. A Hugo Boss billboard sliding by. BADEN-BADEN. The hills to the east hazy, heating up. Paragliders – one, two, three. Boss again – so sleek. Another brief glimpse of the blue-green hills. We jolt to a standstill with a screech. I stare at the sign on the platform outside. BADEN-BADEN.

This was a town I remembered very well. Not this cluster of squat German buildings down by the Rhine, which was just a railway station like any other, but Baden-Baden itself, up in the beech- and oak-covered hills behind the man in Boss jeans. I even remembered the paragliders, spiralling down slowly out of the blue like drunken butterflies.

Gazing out at the half-empty platform, I could clearly picture the morning the previous summer when my bus had left the roar of the truck-clogged highway along the Rhine and swept into the long, curving tunnel through those hills towards Baden-Baden. A few minutes later we'd emerged, like lost children in a storybook, in an enchanted village a hundred years earlier – perhaps even two hundred, depending on where your glance fell.

For those first few moments, left standing with my suitcase on the cobbles in the sunny quiet, I'd felt locked in a spell. Empty, crooked streets. A castle on a crag. A clock striking twelve, then silence. For just a fraction of a second I would not have been in the least astonished if Dostoyevsky himself had bolted out of a side-street, unshaven and smelling of onions, on his way to the pawnbroker's with one of his wife's rings. It had felt curiously like *déjà vu* – I'd never been there in my life. Then a young man talking Turkish into a mobile phone had come striding round the corner and my head had cleared.

Although I wouldn't have knocked one back, I had not come to Baden-Baden that summer to see ghosts. I had come simply to smell old Russia. Every Russian writer I loved had once visited or lived here – they'd all been great travellers. I'm not sure what I thought that looking at the streets they'd walked in, the hotels they'd stayed in or the casino tables they'd played at might give me. Like any tourist, I've often stood with a group of other blank-faced foreigners in some museum or medieval palace, staring at a bed an illustrious king or poet or navigator died in, wondering where I might later have lunch or why someone with the legs of the Frenchman in front of me would choose to wear shorts. What are we supposed to *do* with the bed some Portuguese king died in centuries ago? 'In 1521, after a long illness, surrounded by his wife and sons . . .' The guide is in full flight, darting in and out of an exhausting variety of European languages as she goes, while we peer at the pristine counterpane, the scrubbed walls, the dust-free floor, the view from the window, each other . . . What we want, at the very least, is soiled pillow-cases, a night-table littered with

4

apothecary's potions, a royal dog snuffling in a corner, a weeping servant and kitchen smells wafting up the stairwell. We want signs of life. We know what the guide means, but in some very real sense it is not *here* that the king died at all. Place evaporates with time. All the same, like all the others in my group, I nose about, hoping to catch the whiff of something, something transporting, something that will catapult me back, rather than the king forward.

As it happens, dropping in to Baden-Baden was a very Russian thing to do. Tsars and tsarinas had done it (the Romanov and Baden dynasties being linked by marriage), grand dukes, princesses, generals and assorted noblemen had done it, as had writers, poets, playwrights and wealthy Russian families touring Western Europe with their retinues of servants. Russian invalids and hypochondriacs had flocked to Baden-Baden for the waters, while gamblers, adventurers and what Dostoyevsky called 'scum' of every description had infested the magnificent casino, Germany's finest. By the late 1860s, without any trouble at all, you could catch a train from Moscow or St Petersburg all the way to Paris, stopping off in Baden-Baden for a few days, or even a month or two, to take the cure, hobnob with the fashionable set, or try your luck at the tables before crossing into France. Nowadays you can get there from Moscow before lunch, and they're coming in droves again, dressed to the nines.

At first glance Baden-Baden seems an unlikely place to catch the whiff of anything except cakes, expensive perfumes, freshly dry-cleaned jackets, and now and again something faintly nose-pinching. Is it the sulphurous spa water? Pine resin? The tang of a million sun-drenched red geraniums? For an hour or so after settling into my little hotel in Eichstrasse, I ambled about the spotless, tranquil streets nearby, enchanted by the displays in the shop windows, Aladdin's caves of softly lit gold jewellery, Persian rugs, Meissen figurines, antique Oriental furniture and finely tailored silk shirts and blouses. Mingling with the drifts of elderly strollers, I felt almost dazed by the succession of luxury boutiques – all the crystal, perfumes, porcelain, silverware, Venetian glass – each one more discreetly exquisite than the last. In Baden-Baden even McDonald's is all marble and art deco lighting.

Dostoyevsky in his novel *The Gambler* a century and a half before me – or at least somebody very like him in a town very like Baden-Baden – was sickened by this vision of virtuous German toil and its rewards. He became utterly enraged by the way the Germans amassed wealth over generations, scraping up money, gulden by gulden, 'like Jews', until they could live in a picture-book house with a stork in the chimney-pot like everyone else's. It made his 'Tartar blood' boil. Russians, he boasted, acquire wealth through taking risks – 'raising hell', as he put it, or 'recklessly staking everything on the roulette wheel' – and then in the most outrageous manner squandering it.

By the time I reached the rivulet (crazy-paved to stop it getting muddy) at the bottom of the hill, I was feeling slightly peevish myself. Even Hermann Hesse, usually the very model of kindly understanding (in a Hindu sort of way), got quite snappish, limping about these same streets in 1923 with his handsome Malacca bamboo cane. What is the purpose of all these bronze lions and lizards and novelty ashtrays, he asks in 'A Guest at the Spa', these pictures of shepherdesses and these Chinese divinities turned into parasol-handles? Why do the middle classes seek out these useless bagatelles? How can they sit, almost unable to breathe, let alone talk, surrounded by the 'thick clotted luxury' of all the marble, silver, rugs and mirrors they've acquired? Feeling desolate and bored, he makes his way back to his spa hotel, where he's taking the cure for his mild sciatica.

Not having quite so salubrious a hotel to take refuge in, I crossed a pretty little bridge, festooned with red geraniums, to the park on the other side and then sauntered off along the river towards the casino – which Hesse had also haunted, as a matter of fact, as had Dostoyevsky and Tolstoy before him.

All of a sudden, from the direction of the casino, I caught the unmistakable strains of a Baden-Baden Bert Kaempfert wafting across the brilliant green lawns, purring something about blueness and eyes and waiting in Mexico. Leaving the crazy-paved river with its little bridges, I headed off across the grass towards the long, white casino with its columned portico, squinting into the late afternoon sun to see exactly where the music was coming from. Right in front of the main entrance a dozen couples, well past middle age, were dancing to 'Spanish Eyes' with spry elegance, so light on their feet they seemed to be half-floating. Loud applause from the smiling crowd of onlookers seated nearby in the sunshine.

As the sun slid down behind the deep-green cloud of trees behind the casino, with our Kaempfert crooning on about love and loss and hope and hopelessness, I felt delectably swathed in melancholy, light years away from the panic-stricken world I'd come from that morning through the tunnel in my little bus.

And then it happened – I began to slide back into a world I knew had never existed.

'ON 10TH AUGUST 1862, at four o'clock in the afternoon, in Baden-Baden, in front of the famous casino, a large crowd of people had gathered. It was delightful weather and everything round about – the green trees, the brightly coloured houses of the cosy town, the gently rolling hills – everything lay spread out in the balmy sunshine brimful with festive feelings . . . Smiles hovered on people's faces, old and young . . .' The opening lines of Ivan Turgenev's novel *Smoke*.

The orchestra on that particular afternoon in 1862, according to Turgenev, was playing Strauss waltzes and a potpourri from *La Traviata*, with the odd Russian romance thrown in to please the many Russians in the crowd – foppishly dressed landowners from the provinces, bleary-eyed, one imagines, from too many late nights at the roulette tables inside; a few princes and counts in pale-coloured gloves and rakishly angled hats; writers, of course, and government clerks on the make; countesses and cocottes; and any number of those sensitive souls, as Turgenev noted with a sneer, in whose arms poor Chopin had expired.

Turgenev's eye then drifted with the dispersing crowd along the nearby Lichtentaler Allee – still one of Europe's most beautiful promenades, in its setting of meadow-like parklands dotted with oaks, liquidambars, beech and huge magnolias along the banks of the mud-free Oos. There, around the *arbre russe*, one of the many chestnut trees in the park, the town's Russians would gather to parade, exchange gossip, court, borrow money and lecture each other, as only Russians can, about what was right and what was outrageously wrong with the world.

Turgenev himself often used to sit on a bench on the Lichtentaler Allee to watch the promenaders strolling up and down beside the river in their finery, engaging this one or that in civilised conversation. Needless to say, it's not the sort of thing that a middle-aged man sitting alone on a park bench can do nowadays without arousing suspicion.

In Turgenev's day things were different. Conversation was such a prized social activity in the middle of the nineteenth century, the art of conversation such a treasured accomplishment, that the casino itself went under the name of *Conversationshaus*. In fact, what Turgenev actually wrote in the opening sentence of *Smoke* was: 'in front of the famous *Conversation* a large crowd of people had gathered'.

I was aware, of course, as I drifted with him through the park, 'Amor, Amor' still echoing in my ears (a good Cuban rhumba just won't go away) that I must not talk to anyone. Even to smile at anyone I passed would have been provocative, a sign of my possibly having mischief on my mind. In fact, we seemed invisible to each other, the other strollers and I, like characters in completely different novels. Occasionally somebody alone and younger would zip past on a skateboard or stride along the path with a terrier on a leash, but for the most part it was just a procession of sedate, stiff-jointed couples well past their prime – most of them, if Hesse is to be believed, engaged in an unrelenting struggle with uric acid and sclerosis. No French governesses making eyes at English lords, no Princess Zizis, Princess Zozos or London lionesses, peering at the passing crowd through elegant lorgnettes, not even any proper riff-raff. At one point a tallish woman in a black wig and full crinolines came tottering past, parasol up, rouged and mascara'd like one of the high-class harlots in *Smoke*, but this was obviously just an embarrassing stab at make-believe – or outright lunacy.

What brought me up short, thrusting me back into the here and now, was abruptly finding myself face to face with a bust of the great writer himself. It had quite recently been placed on a waist-high plinth near the old *arbre russe* by the Ministry of Culture of the Russian Federation. His handsome, bearded face, now a dull green, was staring with unseeing eyes at Brenner's Park-Hotel and Spa across the river, as lifeless as a stuffed moose.

IVAN TURGENEV

1818–1883

BADEN-BADEN

1863–1870

To tell the truth, I never much fancied Turgenev when I was young. In fact, when I first began reading Russian novels as a student in my late teens, I scarcely noticed he was there. At eighteen or nineteen, on the basis of almost no experience at all in any department of life, you naturally feel drawn, I think, to writers who reflect your own deeply rooted certainties – or who will at least turn your uncertainties, your anxieties and anger, into fireworks, lighting up the sky. What you want is Dostoyevsky and Tolstoy. You want *Crime and Punishment* and *The Brothers Karamazov*, you want *Anna Karenina* and *War and Peace*. In other words, you want vast, powerful whirlpools you can plunge into, even at the risk of drowning – not a pond. You want a symphony, not a sonata, you crave something that will sweep you up, time after time, something that will make your soul take flight. If you have a whit of imagination at that age, you want to tumble about with Napoleon and axe-murderers and visions of God, not hang about in musty drawing-rooms, as Turgenev's readers are often forced to do, watching some scion of the petty gentry fret over whether his

11

beloved really has a headache, as she claims, or won't leave her bed because she doesn't love him any more. Turgenev seemed far too prim to me then, his novels such as *Fathers and Sons* or even *On the Eve* too full of fruitless dithering. He seemed, in a word, far too virginal, as I was myself.

At the other end of my life, naturally enough, I read with an ear for sensibilities of a quite different kind. Turgenev's delicate sonatas are now much more appealing. The idea of sitting quietly beside one of his dreamy ponds, or even in one of his musty drawing-rooms, eavesdropping on rambling conversations about all the things that really matter in life, now fills me with deep pleasure. He irritates me occasionally, both as a man and a writer, as somebody you feel you've drawn close to can. He shamelessly shilly-shallied, he could be annoyingly aloof – he was an aristocrat, after all, and always liked to take his own time. But there's a large-heartedness about the man and his works which you can't help strongly warming to. And his Russian is incomparably beautiful. (Not counting Pushkin's, of course – Pushkin's is beyond discussion.)

For me at eighteen, understandably, this was not nearly enough.

———

It's a fine head, Turgenev's – *une belle tête*, as the French would put it, covering rather more ground than we do in English with those three short words. Green and blind, but undeniably imposing. I studied him at my leisure from my vantage point a few paces away seated on the *Turgenev Bank am Russischen Baum,* as the small, bronze memorial plaque on the back of the bench announced it to be. Large, with a long, slightly fleshy nose, deep-set eyes, strong cheekbones, thick, kempt beard. A handsome head. Indeed, he was a strikingly handsome man, by all accounts, even when he was no longer young, at least according to the notions of his time. Even today, probably. The only jarring note was his voice: oddly high-pitched, we're told (by almost everybody), not at all the booming bass you might have expected from such a tall, deep-chested man . . . and so (although hardly anybody said this too directly) uncomfortably effeminate – one more reason for Dostoyevsky to loathe him.

———

Not one of the passing crowd of promenaders spared Turgenev so much as a glance. He was just another bust in a public place. It's doubtful whether many of them, even the better-read, let alone the skateboarders, could have named a single novel he'd written. *Fathers and Sons*, the world's first novel about a nihilist (who contrives to fall in love), might have rung a bell in a few cases, but only a faint one, I suspect. Would I even have found his novels – Russia's first modern European novels of any consequence: *Rudin*, *A Nest of the Gentry*, *On the Eve*, or *Smoke*, written right here in Baden-Baden – in the local bookshop?

When Turgenev sat here on the Lichtentaler Allee in the 1860s, enjoying the passing cavalcade, he was Russia's most celebrated novelist. Dostoyevsky and Tolstoy, it's true, were catching up fast – their first masterpieces (*Crime and Punishment*, *The Idiot*, *War and Peace*) came out while Turgenev was living in Baden-Baden, writing very little – but everyone he doffed his hat to in those years, even those Russians who thought that every word he'd written was a calumny on their native land (the nobility, the social order, the revolutionary intelligentsia – some section of Russian society was always incensed by what he wrote), would have recognised the elegantly attired man on the bench by the river as an international literary celebrity, at home in the best drawing-rooms from London to Moscow. And absolutely everyone strolling past, whether or not they'd read a word of what he'd written, would have known that right there under their noses in Baden-Baden this affable Russian landowner was living in a highly irregular triangular sort of arrangement – *ménage à trois,* trio, troika, call it what you will – with the French opera singer Pauline Viardot and her husband Louis. And that this intriguing triangle formed the very summit of Baden-Baden's glittering social life.

And now – almost total eclipse. It was curious.

Across the river from where I was sitting, beneath a bright, greening sky, the windows of Brenner's Park-Hotel and Spa were starting to glow amber and gold. There was a twilight feeling in the park. It was time for me to go looking for Ilse.

———

One steamy morning at Colombo Railway Station, waiting for the Hikkaduwa train to leave, I sat idly trying to fix the zipper on my leather travelling bag. It must have been in about 1976, when, experiencing a mild attack of Chekhovian panic about being married, I flew off to Sri Lanka for a month on my own, somewhere gentle and utterly foreign where all the familiar landmarks in my life would find no echo.

Whatever I was seeking in Sri Lanka, it was the broken zipper which turned the journey into an adventure. The German woman sitting opposite me in the railway carriage offered to help me fix it. We started to chat, as you can with a friendly fellow-traveller you don't think you'll ever see again, and, when I ran into her and her husband on the beach at Hikkaduwa the next morning, I began to be aware of those little bursts of intimacy – of recognition and a desire for no good reason to know more – which turn merely liking somebody into friendship.

A couple of weeks later we found ourselves quite by chance at the same hotel in Negombo. And in the years that have followed we've met up many times on both sides of the world – Sydney, Melbourne, Munich, Berlin – we write, we telephone; she even came to live in Australia for some years, as did her husband. Ilse was now coming to Baden-Baden for a couple of days to meet up with me. She would look breathtakingly elegant – I could picture the long mid-season coat, the silk scarf at her throat, the tasteful jewellery from Berlin. First we would sit over coffee and cake talking about a thousand things and laughing a lot, then, next morning, we would set out in search of traces of the world I'd spent half my life trying to seize hold of: the world Tolstoy, Dostoyevsky and Turgenev had lived in.

In particular, I was thinking as I made my way out of the park that I'd rather like to bring the green bust on the Lichtentaler Allee alive. But how? How could wandering around Baden-Baden with a friend from Berlin who almost certainly knew very little about Turgenev help me do that? Of course, in Ilse's company, at least in my experience, almost anything was possible.

No sooner had I taken my seat at the little table in the forecourt of the Europäischer Hof to wait for her – it's one of those vast nine-teenth-century establishments on the banks of the Oos, opposite the casino – than I found myself staring at a plaque on the wall beside me which read:

Unter vielen hochrangigen russischen Gästen
lebte hier im Sommer 1862 auch
Irina Ratmirova, Heldin des Romans 'Rauch' von
IVAN S. TURGENEV
(1818–1883)

(Among many other high-ranking Russian guests staying
here in the summer of 1862 was
Irina Ratmirova, heroine of the novel 'Smoke'
by Ivan S. Turgenev 1818–1883)

But she *wasn't* – Irina never existed, she's a character in a novel! It's true that a woman called Alexandra Dolgorukaya once existed, Alexander II's mistress, lady-in-waiting to the tsarina and wife of General Albedinsky, and it's true that Turgenev had *la Grande Demoiselle*, as she was called, very much in mind when he wrote *Smoke*. But there had never been any Irina Ratmirova. It's the phrase 'among many other high-ranking Russian guests' that is mischievous, in my opinion, conjuring up images of an actual guest from Russia called Irina Ratmirova alighting from carriages at the entrance, walking up and down the grand staircase and even appearing from time to time on one of the geranium-garlanded balconies overlooking the river. (In any case, the hotel had no balconies in 1862 – indeed, the whole layout of the Hôtel de l'Europe, as it was called then, was different in Turgenev's day.)

When I pointed this out to Ilse, almost as soon as she arrived, she flew inside immediately to remonstrate with the receptionist. She does this kind of thing. While she argued in vehement tones about the absurdity of claiming that a Frau Ratmirova had ever stayed there – '*sie*

*kann gar nicht in diesem Hotel gelebt haben, verstehen Sie, weil sie nie
existiert hat – es gab keine Irina Ratmirova!'* – I pretended to be
engrossed in the list of other high-ranking guests which was hanging
by the front door: Prince William of Prussia, some Russian chancellor
or other, Liszt, Rossini, Haile Selassie, Jimmy Carter . . . Behind me, Ilse
had reached an impasse with the receptionist, who was courteous but
unmoved. Perhaps, she said, since we were interested in Turgenev, we
would like to look around the hotel?

I could see that Ilse now thought the whole establishment was a
sham, but I couldn't resist. The staircase, for instance, which the hero
and heroine of *Smoke* had flown up and down, half-crazed with guilty
passion, was just along the corridor to the right. No, there had never
been any Irina Ratmirova, nor any Grigory Litvinov, for that matter, to
fly up and down anything, or to have trysts in a suite on the second
floor, not to mention the luggage room opposite (where scandalously
inappropriate fumblings had taken place while Irina's husband was
dressing for dinner . . . 'Do as you wish . . . I am yours . . . I will do
anything') – I knew that. All the same, I clearly had to see the staircase.

It was vast, as I had hoped, with Tuscan red walls on the landings at
each level, glimpsed between huge, white Greek columns. These
columns struck me as vulgar and out of place, although in Irina's day
there had been a columned portico at the original front entrance leading directly to the staircase, so perhaps they hadn't jarred on Irina. In
any case, in Turgenev's opinion, if *Smoke* is any guide, few of the
Russians who frequented Baden-Baden in the early 1860s would have
recognised vulgarity if you'd rubbed their noses in it. I stood at a bend
in the staircase by one of the naked nymphs holding a lantern and tried
to imagine Irina and Grigory trudging up the stairs in utter despair or
floating down them on a cloud of amorous feelings, sneaking up them

to avoid being caught – it was a hothouse of intrigue and assignations, the Hôtel de l'Europe, in its day – or descending with a noisy crowd of other Russians to dine in style downstairs.

While Ilse inspected the sumptuous reception rooms below, I stood transported, at least momentarily. I could see the lace, the shawls, the gloves, the modish shoes peeping out from under long satin dresses, I could hear the chatter, the daring rise and fall of Russian conversation (so unlike flat English), the clink of good silver on fine china in the dining-room below. Standing there, I could understand – or at least begin to – why Irina and Grigory talked and behaved in the extraordinary way they did.

———

To be frank, *Smoke* is not a very good novel. Perhaps I should phrase that a little differently: few nowadays are accustomed to take pleasure in a novel like *Smoke*. It is (from my point of view) a deliciously old-fashioned novel, with an intrusive, rather cantankerous, omniscient narrator, about a nice young Russian landowner called Grigory Litvinov who, while waiting in Baden-Baden for his fiancée, Tatyana, to join him, runs across an old flame of his, Irina Ratmirova, now a stuffy general's wife, who had once cruelly betrayed him, and . . . well, you could almost write the rest of it yourself: sparks fly. But right at the very end Litvinov marries his saintlike, infinitely tedious fiancée after all. Or at least he seems doomed to marry her: since this is Turgenev and Turgenev always loses interest in the storyline once marriage seems a certainty, Grigory and Tatyana are left to get themselves to the altar without his assistance. ('But it's time to finish,' Turgenev writes unceremoniously, just as we've got to the point where, after years of sullen separation, Grigory bounds into Tatyana's drawing-room, falls at her feet and begins to kiss the hem of her dress. 'Anyway, there's no point in adding anything. My readers can work it out for themselves. Now, what about Irina?' Ah, yes, still miserably attached to that general – much more interesting.)

Could this tale be transposed to the Baden-Baden I was visiting? Could you really 'write the rest of it yourself'? Could, for instance, any of the youthful crowd in bomber-jackets, singlets and chunky boots in McDonald's ever come up with a story like *Smoke*? Or, for that matter, the exquisitely dressed matrons sipping their glasses of white wine on the Leopoldsplatz? Indeed, could I? (Could Ilse?) We, too, fall in love, of course. We get engaged, make vows, rekindle old flames, commit adultery, betray and find ourselves betrayed – none of the nodal elements in the narrative are strange to us. Yet something about Turgenev's narrative is not of our time.

Take 'betrayal', for example, the concept the novel's whole storyline is based on. In reality, a century and a half after Irina Ratmirova stayed at the Hôtel de l'Europe, post-Jung, post-Freud, post- almost everything, most of us would find it difficult to imagine ourselves back into a world where betrayal meant what it meant to the characters in *Smoke*. In finding different words for the situations they faced, I think we would also end up with different characters – and, eventually, different situations.

When they are teenagers in Moscow, for instance, just before the Crimean War, Irina betrays her promise to marry Litvinov. Leaving a rather scrappy note of apology ('Forgive me, Grigory . . . I am suffering dreadfully, but it is done . . . it must be my fate . . . I am not worthy of you' – the usual concoction of clichés from novels she's been reading), she takes up a better offer of escape from her impoverished family than anything the faintly dull Litvinov can provide and is swept off in a wealthy count's carriage to St Petersburg. Ten years later in Baden-Baden, now a general's wife and society belle, she battens on to him again although she knows perfectly well that he is not 'free'. After a flurry of breathless notes and breathless visits to each other's hotels, a *rendez-vous* or two on the Lichtentaler Allee and a multitude of protestations of love, all far too highly perfumed for our taste, she seduces him. (' "Tell me, do you love me?" She took him in her arms and pressed his head to her breast, her comb fell to the floor with a tinkle, and her loosened hair flowed over him in a soft, sweet-smelling wave . . .') This act of adultery, by the way, occurs at his hotel, not hers, although we're never told which hotel Litvinov is staying at. Certainly, if we knew, we'd be beating a path to its door in droves, demanding to see the exact spot where that comb hit the floor.

Needless to say, once the change in Litvinov's affections becomes official, his wholesome angel of a fiancée is packed off smartly, on the verge of a nervous breakdown, back to Russia. Irina then changes her mind about eloping with Litvinov to Spain, having taken a saner look at her prospects, and so he also leaves for Russia, also on the verge of a nervous breakdown. (' "Smoke, smoke," he repeated to himself several times. And suddenly everything appeared to be smoke, everything, his own life, Russian life – everything human . . .') Betrayal, as you can see, at every turn. Only the virtuous Russian virgin, Tatyana, betrays no one. Betrayal is not in her vocabulary, although not for the reason it's not in the skateboarders' or the wine-sippers'.

At the core of what is betrayed in *Smoke* is duty – one's duty to keep one's word and to uphold the established moral code. Fine, upstanding citizens broke the established moral code at every opportunity, naturally, but only in established ways. 'If we don't recognise duty, then what do we have left?' Tatyana's aunt berates Litvinov. It's not his dalliance with a married woman she's aghast at – at least, not the dalliance in itself. Who didn't dally with married women? What has left her tearful and quivering is Litvinov's desire to break off the engagement to her niece – and for the trivial reason that he and Tatyana would not be happy together. (As if one married for happiness!) 'Giving in to your own whims without considering other people ... what sort of freedom is that?' A very common sort, I'd have thought.

I can't be sure of the attitude to duty of the young men I saw skating past me along the Lichtentaler Allee, but I doubt they would agree that there's nothing left if you ignore it. In fact, if they were assailed by Tatyana's aunt in similar circumstances, they'd probably wonder what exactly the old duck thought they had a duty *to*. To upholding the rules? What rules? If we could all agree on the rules, then breaking them might not be the confusing business it is these days. It's like cheating at poker: first you have to admit you're playing poker. Nowadays, unlike Litvinov and Irina, few of us can agree what game we're playing. We're on much surer ground ticking off what obligations others have to us – our rights, in other words. In the absence of moral codes we take refuge in laws.

Turgenev himself, by the way, didn't betray anyone in his amorous peregrinations, as far as I can tell, although not because duty was uppermost in his mind. He was guided in his affairs by an idea of love even more foreign to most of us than Litvinov's or Tatyana's and was true to it, on the whole, from the moment he first met Pauline Viardot until the day he died.

Very little is foreign to Ilse: she is the purest dilettante I have ever encountered, astounding me every time we meet with the stories of her wanderings – her *vagabondages*, as the French might say more revealingly – geographical, of course, in the sense of darting about the globe, but also intellectual and spiritual. In all her wanderings, however, it turned out that she'd only ever come across Ivan Turgenev as a name people tack on to any list of great Russian writers. She certainly couldn't recall having read any of his books.

What I first wanted to tell her about was not his irregular love life, although I knew she'd be all ears, but his language. This seemed the best place to start delving into what I found fascinating about Turgenev: the richness of his – and his characters' – vocabulary for every permutation of desire, passion, frustration, anger, grief and joy.

Every note Irina and Litvinov write to each other, for instance, is a modest work of art, every conversation a reflection of their awareness of the array of nuances Russian offers through subtle games with word order, rhythm, prefixes, suffixes and, of course, its vast vocabulary. Not that anybody would have imagined in 1867, when the novel appeared, that this was how real people spoke and wrote to each other. It was perfectly plain to educated readers in those days that this was art, not life, that this was Turgenev displaying his mastery of the language, not the record of what two real people might actually have said to each other. How easily Turgenev's kind of finespun writing passes into our language depends on the translation, naturally, but I suspect it will often strike us nowadays as falsely genteel or impossibly purple.

Perhaps the precise difference between 'passion', say, and 'adoration' hardly matters. Does it matter whether I call myself 'infatuated' or 'smitten'? To write *'amour'* instead of 'love affair' is surely just an affectation, isn't it? It only matters, it seems to me, in the sense that it matters if 'red' is the only word we have to describe that whole spectrum of colours from coral pink to burgundy. To go through life not knowing 'vermilion', 'scarlet', 'cerise', 'magenta', 'puce' – there are dozens of them – is to go through life half-blind. Knowing all these words, the 'salmon pinks', the 'fuchsias', the 'garnets' and the 'carmines', allows us to ponder choices not open to somebody who just knows 'red' – 'ponder' being the vital word here. It allows us to exercise our will over what is given. More importantly, it allows us to turn the ordinariness of our everyday lives into something, if not extraordinary, then at least poetic. Poetry, however, like flirtation, is not something we have much time for nowadays. We seem only to have time for seduction, for reading the signposts to fulfilment. We like to wrap things up and move on. Ilse and I that evening, I remember, seemed to have all the time in the world.

Whatever the limitations in our emotional vocabulary today, we have at least deconstructed that pesky word 'love'. A century and a half ago Litvinov could still claim he was looking for 'love' – at least he was convinced that he'd 'fallen in love' with Irina, once 'loved' her and now 'loved' her again. I presume by 'love' he meant that strange, vivifying and also comforting *mélange* of sexual and emotional intimacy, excitement, contentment, friendship, companionship, respect and trust which appears like a mirage on almost everybody's path once puberty is well under way, even today, at least where I come from. It tends to separate out, of course, as time passes, which is why we have the novel, but deceptively, at the beginning, it's usually a very smooth blend indeed.

———

Irina was looking for 'love' as well – or so she said. ('Do you love me? Do you love me?' . . . 'My love for you has replaced everything else.') Actually what she wanted, as a modern-day Litvinov would discern in a flash if he had his wits about him, was not love at all, but rescuing. Irina wanted to be saved – quite understandably, and who apart from a man could do it? – first from her shamefully impoverished family in Moscow ('Love me, love me, my darling, my saviour') and then ten years later in Baden-Baden from her vapid life as a society belle surrounded by overdressed cretins ('Save me, pull me from this abyss I'm in before it destroys me!'). Twice, in other words, for a short time at least, Litvinov looked as if he might come in handy as a saviour, but in the end Irina yearned to be saved with the sort of panache and grandeur he could never offer. One gavotte at a ball in Madrid (if they'd ever got as far as eloping to Spain) and Litvinov would have found himself reading precisely the same letter of dismissal, written from some Spanish marquis's country estate, which was sent to him from the Hôtel de l'Europe in Baden-Baden. At the beginning of the twenty-first century it's hard to believe that a sophisticated couple like Irina and Litvinov would not have unpacked the 'love' package within the first few weeks, perhaps even days, into its component parts, leaving a present-day Turgenev with an interesting mess to describe, perhaps, but not the finely choreographed dance we find in *Smoke*.

In the event, Ilse and I ended up skirting around the subject of love and betrayal when we got to it, not, I think, out of any sense of delicacy, but because over the last twenty-five years or so we'd had occasion to discuss such things all too often.

Setting off to find something to eat in the spa quarter beyond the main square, we passed the house Gogol had once lived in on the Jesuitenplatz, as well as Dostoyevsky's house in Bäderstrasse, now Coco's, an interior design shop, with a bronze bust of Dostoyevsky stuck high up on the wall, half-hidden by geraniums. By the time we'd chosen somewhere to sit out the evening, we'd more or less decided that the next day we'd go in search of the two houses in which Turgenev had spent his Baden-Baden years – in the shadow, always, of his great love, the very pivot of his being, the celebrated diva Pauline Viardot-García. And her husband.

From the moment he first heard her sing in St Petersburg in *The Barber of Seville* in October 1843 until he died, almost literally in her arms, exactly forty years later in the chalet he'd built behind her house in Bougival near Paris, Turgenev was possessed, body and soul, by the famous mezzo-soprano Pauline Viardot-García. Or perhaps he was merely smitten when he heard her sing and fell in love when, after befriending her husband Louis on a hunting trip, he went to visit her at her apartment on the Nevsky Prospekt on 13 November.

Although at that time, apart from being good-looking, he had little to recommend him – as Pauline later said herself, he was just 'a young Russian landowner, a good shot, an agreeable conversationalist and a bad poet' (worse: a 'fatuous dandy', according to Herzen) – he was soon invited to join the select group of admirers admitted to her dressing-room after her performances. There in the softly lit, heated room beneath the stage she would receive Turgenev and his three fervent rivals, seating each of them on one paw of the magnificent bearskin they'd brought her, the bear's claws now replaced with claws of gold. As Virginia Woolf cruelly remarked, this paw was to become his permanent lodging. Viardot herself seems to have sat somewhere in the middle in a white lace *peignoir*, although it's hard to picture how she did this gracefully. Nowadays I expect we'd call such a scene high camp, but in 1843 it was just deliciously theatrical. They knew how to do things in those days. He was twenty-five and she was twenty-two, and he was hers forever.

Over the ensuing forty years he had other liaisons, naturally, from fleeting sexual encounters to serious infatuations and loving friend-ships. The rock his life was founded on, however, from the moment she appeared on the stage of the Bolshoi Kamenny Theatre in St Petersburg until the day of his death, was Pauline Viardot-García. I don't imagine an hour went by during all those years when his thoughts did not hover around and then alight upon the image of this beloved woman – her fiery, hooded eyes, sooty black, her large mouth and her shiny black hair, drawn back severely in a parting from her high, white forehead.

Yet all the words I might find to describe this love somehow miss the mark. To call it a 'great love affair' makes it sound oddly banal, as if he and Viardot were lovers, which, as far as anybody knows for cer-tain, they were not. To say he was 'deeply in love' with her all his life makes him sound eternally frustrated in his feelings, even adolescent, yet for most of his life it was a stable, enriching love. It was not just a matter of 'passion', either, although there was ardour there of a kind, especially in the early years. Nor was it merely disembodied 'adoration' – in letter after letter he kissed her hands and her feet (although not her lips). In some of his letters to women he was smitten by he went further, but the kissing is an indication that his feelings for Pauline were more than simply friendly, there was desire there, too, especially at first. Perhaps it was a poetic kind of madness, an incurable roman-tic illness triggered by a night at the opera.

One thing seems obvious to me: a love such as this is only possible between two points in a triangle. Otherwise there will be thunder and lightning and what links the two lovers will eventually break asunder. The third point may be a husband or wife or it may be something else entirely.

Quite possibly there is no name at all for this kind of love. Perhaps, in fact, there is no need for a name since so few of us will ever experience anything like it. For the lives most of us lead, the old words will almost certainly do, one replacing the other as the years go by. On the other hand, if I could find the right word for what Turgenev felt, perhaps the love my own life is rooted in would grow even more luxuriantly.

I want to know what it felt like to love someone like that. I want to find the words.

———

What was unforgivable about this love – and few forgave it – was not the fact that Pauline Viardot was married (to the scholar, twenty years her senior, Louis Viardot, the former director of the Théâtre Italien in Paris). What was unforgivable was her ugliness. In a travel diary, published years later as *A European Journal,* the Englishwoman Mary Wilson, who saw Pauline perform at the Berlin Opera in 1847, called her 'personally hideous beyond compare'. The German poet Heinrich Heine tried to be a little kinder: yes, she was ugly, he wrote, 'but with the kind of ugliness which is noble'. Trying to put his finger on what it was about the diva that so captured the attention, he had recourse to expressions such as 'the terrifying splendour of some exotic, wild land'. When she opens her large mouth to sing, he wrote, 'we feel as if the most monstrous plants and animals from India and Africa are about to appear before our eyes, giant palms festooned with thousands of blossoming lianas', leopards, giraffes, 'even a herd of young elephants'. Heine was, of course, a Romantic.

When I look now at the portrait painted of her at the age of twenty, I see a sullen young gypsy, not inelegant – well, she has been posed and lit to her advantage – but noticeably plain-featured. A scullery-maid with pretensions and the temperament to cause havoc. The photograph taken of her at forty-seven in Baden-Baden, seated at the piano, shows a strikingly unprepossessing woman – masculine, squat and double-chinned. To this day Russians mutter darkly about this 'witch' who put their great writer under a spell, dragging him across Europe to her castle at Courtavenel outside Paris – and it was a real medieval castle, too, with turrets and a moat – where she turned him into a foreigner. If she'd been 'beautiful', I wonder if they'd have been more inclined to forgive her?

———

Just a few minutes' walk from my little hotel in Eichstrasse, tucked in behind the towering neogothic Evangelical Church with its maddening chiming clock, is the street Turgenev first found rooms in when he moved to Baden-Baden in 1863 to be with the Viardots – at Pauline's suggestion. Twenty years after they'd first met on her Russian tour, and after some difficult years of separation, they'd found, it seems, a new, remarkably happy way of loving each other.

The town must have seemed to him then – well, it did to me that morning – like a fairytale come true. Green, picturesque, tranquil, rich, cosmopolitan, there it nestled on the banks of its crystal stream, a magnet for Europe's upper crust, yet at the same time so secluded that history always seemed to be taking place somewhere else, far beyond the ring of bluish hills. Napoleon III's dictatorship in France, the chaos in Russia, the attacks from every side over his most recent novel (*Fathers and Sons* – in fact, he had been savagely attacked over almost everything he'd ever written) – all this must have seemed as remote as the civil war in Mexico. He would be able to spend his mornings here, he must have thought, peacefully writing book after book – after all, in 1863 he was still Russia's most famous living writer, if not its most loved. Of an afternoon he could stroll on the Lichtentaler Allee, doffing his hat to the passing *haut monde*, or sit in a café arguing with Russian students up from Heidelberg for a bit of high life. There would be plenty of hunting in the woods with friends, too – Turgenev had a lifelong passion for killing animals and birds. There would be concerts, picnics and dinners in sumptuous restaurants with original masterpieces glowing in the candlelight on the walls behind him.

Mostly, however, it was a fairytale because, in the first place, it was not Russia and, in the second place, because Pauline, virtually queen of Baden-Baden society (even the King of Prussia came to hear her sing), was living just around the corner and up the hill. Indeed, once he'd built himself his own villa next door to hers, he could see her several times a day. The Baden-Baden years turned out to be the happiest of his life. It may not have been happiness of the kind he'd dreamt of as a youth or while sitting on those gilded bear's claws, he still felt he'd 'missed out on the main prize in life's lottery' (family happiness), but he was certainly more contented than he'd ever been before.

THE ILLUSION OF A FAIRYTALE was hard for Ilse and me to hold on to that particular morning. At breakfast in the sun in the Leopoldsplatz our eyes kept coming to rest on the newspaper headlines from the tumultuous wider world. Terror groups, car-bombings, hijackings, preparations for war – it was pandemonium out there, although on the Leopoldsplatz at that hour, apart from the occasional dog-walker or shop-keeper unlocking his door, nothing was stirring. The chaos in the headlines was all too *big* for us that morning, so we tried to find smaller things, right-sized things, to talk about to give us a sense of the rightness, and even goodness, of that moment there together in that café. It's odd how catastrophe can make you seek comfort in the smaller, more ordinary things – dead-heading the roses, playing ball with the dog, reading an old Agatha Christie novel, chatting about nothing in particular with a friend on the phone – but often it does. In the end it's probably the small things, not the big ones, like seismic shifts in history or life-changing epiphanies, which keep us afloat.

It's always been a delicate balancing act, dealing with the cataclysms of the previous day in the newspaper over breakfast. On the one hand there are shipwrecks, mining disasters and assassinations, not to mention the catalogue of more minor miseries such as suicides and bankruptcies, while on the other there's the irritation of the marmalade running out or of spilling the sugar on the carpet. Turning the shipwrecks into riveting short stories and the spilt sugar into an absorbing drama, we hope the world will seem less out of joint.

We were still talking about small things – Ilse's husband's new passion for golf, the strange pinging sound in the ceiling above my bed at the hotel – as we turned into Schillerstrasse beside the Evangelical Church, hardly a stone's throw, really, from the Leopoldsplatz. It was idyllic. Down one side stretched nineteenth-century apartment houses in carved brown stone, while on the other, behind flower-beds ablaze with colour, stood Brenner's Park-Hotel and Spa, the sort of establishment where liveried footmen must surely appear at your side before you even quite realise you need one. It was the kind of street in which Ilse was every inch at home and I would once have liked to be.

Somewhere here was where Turgenev had lived for several years while he was building his villa. I knew we'd find nothing, I knew that Number 7 had long since been demolished, all the books made it quite clear that Frau Anstett's house where he'd had rooms on the first floor, argued with Dostoyevsky, become a German and finally tasted happiness, had long since gone. Yet I wanted to come into the presence of something.

The modern Number 7 is inhabited by some doctor now, a *Badearzt*, as are half the houses in the town. Baden-Baden is all spa physicians, chiropractors and ayurveda clinics from one end of town to the other, catering as it does to the same crowds of the half-well as it did in Hesse's day. Knowing that this was not the house, knowing the numbers had been changed, we still stood and looked at it. The churchbell clanged ten. We stood and stared. Then, a little further on, we came to a block of luxury apartments, the *Residenz Turgenjew*, set back from the street in a pink sea of petunias. Perhaps this was where Frau Anstett's house had once stood. Perhaps up there in the air above the petunias was where Turgenev on that infamous summer's day in 1867 had offered Dostoyevsky a cutlet (the great man was in the middle of his lunch when Dostoyevsky arrived), and then the bickering had started, Dostoyevsky had become abusive and hysterical as usual and . . . But what did it mean even to think like that? Turgenev had never sat up in the air above these petunias, he had never lived *here* at all. *Here* is always *now*. How can it be anything else?

Nevertheless – despite catching the look in Ilse's eye – I was electrified. There may be no such thing as a ghost, but there was a would-be ghost in the street that morning: me. Given Ivan Sergeyevich's propensity for seeing spectres and revenants, I was surprised he'd never mentioned looking down from his window around ten one summer's morning and seeing *me* hovering in the street below.

NOBODY SEEMS TO KNOW for certain why Dostoyevsky went to see Turgenev at 7 Schillerstrasse at lunchtime on 10 July 1867. Perhaps it was to repay the fifty thalers he'd owed him for several years. Or perhaps it was in the secret hope of squeezing a few more thalers out of the old boy to throw away at the roulette table that afternoon – he was after all in the grip of a gambling frenzy, that summer in Baden-Baden. Possibly he'd simply been on his way to the pawnbroker's with another bundle of his wife's clothes and suddenly felt like 'raising hell'. Visiting Turgenev always made his blood boil.

So, if there were a moment I'd have chosen to haunt Frau Anstett's house, it would have been the moment at noon that day when Dostoyevsky (badly dressed, his beard a tangle, I can just see it) knocked on the door to Turgenev's rooms. I would have liked to see the look on the two men's faces as the door opened: the quiver of resentment on Dostoyevsky's as, taking in Turgenev's foppish attire and the valet lurking in the background, he smelt the delicious, leisurely lunch he'd just interrupted; and the insincere welcoming smile on Turgenev's as he leant forward to receive a kiss on both cheeks. ('I detest his aristocratic, pharisaical way . . . of advancing on you to embrace you,' Dostoyevsky wrote later in a letter to a friend, 'and then presenting his cheek for you to kiss.')

Whatever his immediate reason for calling on the Great Writer, Dostoyevsky had probably been looking for weeks for a pretext to vent his contempt in person for both Turgenev and his work. Obviously he considered *Smoke* to be an outrageous attack on everything he held dear (Russia and the Church), but he'd actually loathed Turgenev for twenty years or more – *Smoke*, which he'd just read, simply added insult to injury. He loathed him partly for the reasons he'd first liked him: 'he's a poet, he's talented, and an aristocrat,' he wrote to his brother after their first meeting, 'superbly handsome, rich, intelligent, educated . . . I can't think of anything nature has denied him.' Dostoyevsky, for his part, had been denied quite a lot – including talent, Turgenev would probably have said in one of his less generous moments. (And he wouldn't be alone, although it's not a fashionable point of view.) While Dostoyevsky had been serving his sentence of four years' hard labour in Siberia, followed by forced military service, Turgenev had either been flitting around Europe having affairs with God knows who – foreign opera stars and Polish noblewomen – or else maundering about his vast estate at Spasskoye, tossing off the odd well-mannered novel about nothing in particular. And he was an atheist – at least he wasn't a Jew – whereas Dostoyevsky was not just a believer: he had returned from Siberia determined that he would 'stay with Christ', as he wrote, 'even if somebody were to prove that Christ is outside truth, and truth really outside Christ'. To Turgenev this sentence would have been pure gobbledygook.

By 1867 Turgenev was in the unsettling position of somebody who has grown accustomed to his own pre-eminence suddenly finding himself elbowed out of the limelight by precisely the young hopefuls he had once condescended to encourage. During the very years he had been doodling in his rooms in Schillerstrasse (to little effect, it must be said – an essay or two, a short story of no account, and the widely reviled *Smoke*) or strolling up and down the Lichtentaler Allee, charming ageing countesses with his witticisms in several languages, Dostoyevsky had written *Notes from Underground* and *Crime and Punishment*, not to mention *The Gambler*, and that lecherous young puritan Leo Tolstoy had begun publishing *War and Peace*, all masterpieces without parallel in Russian, even perhaps European, literature. It's true that Turgenev had once generously called Tolstoy 'the only hope our literature has', but that had been well before his prediction had started to come true.

Here now was this rather scruffy ex-convict, inveterate gambler and religious fanatic barging into his peaceful, sunlit apartment shouting abuse at him. Dostoyevsky claimed later to have remained 'calm and ironical' throughout, which is difficult to imagine. By the same token, Turgenev probably did not 'listen to this philippic in silence', as he, Turgenev, alleged, in the face of Dostoyevsky's insults. He was in fact usually all too quick to lose his head when under attack and may indeed have been brimming over with 'bitterness and bile' that day, as Dostoyevsky's wife later alleged.

At any rate, at some point Dostoyevsky clearly let fly with an attack on *Smoke*: he was incensed by the lines in the novel about Russia's barbarism, the assertion that Russia's only contribution to civilisation had been 'the samovar, the bast shoe, the shaft-bow yoke and the knout – and even they were invented by somebody else'. If Russia were to sink without trace, one of the characters in the novel suggests (Potugin, who, like Turgenev, believes in nothing except 'civilisation'), taking everything Russians had ever invented with her, the rest of humanity wouldn't miss a thing – not a nail or a pin. You couldn't say that even about the Sandwich Islands, Potugin sneers – at least the brutish Polynesians had come up with their own kind of boat and a few spears. Holy Russia no better than some heathenish splodge on the map like the Sandwich Islands? Dostoyevsky was enraged.

'You should get yourself a telescope,' Dostoyevsky remarked acidly.

'A telescope?' Turgenev said, caught off balance. 'What for?'

'Because Russia is such a long way from here,' Dostoyevsky replied ('calmly', he assures us). 'Train your telescope on Russia, why don't you, and then you mightn't find it so hard to see us.'

Touché! Turgenev was appalled, but his opponent had scored a bull's-eye. While his servant cleared away the remains of his cutlet and the Bordeaux (I'm guessing – Turgenev wasn't a drinker and may have settled for a glass of something local), he began lecturing Dostoyevsky on the debt his generation owed to German thinkers. In his youth, after all, he himself had been a student in Berlin. Dostoyevsky retorted that the Germans were nothing but a bunch of dullards, cheats and swindlers and got up to leave.

'That's a personal insult!' Turgenev cried – from his doorway, I like to think, as Dostoyevsky clattered down the stairs. 'You must realise that I have settled here for good, that I regard myself as a German, not a Russian, and that I'm proud of it.' Seething with indignation, Dostoyevsky bolted out into the street and disappeared. If he'd meant to repay his debt, he didn't – he left with the fifty thalers still rattling around in his pocket. He seethed for four whole years over Turgenev's apostasy – to deny one's Russianness, to reject Orthodoxy, was nothing less – and then skewered him with breathtaking cruelty in *The Devils*. Turgenev was wounded to the quick.

IT'S A FAMOUS, FLAMBOYANTLY RUSSIAN quarrel. I knew about it long before I knew anything much about either Dostoyevsky or Turgenev, let alone where Baden-Baden was. It was only one of Ivan Sergeyevich's many bitter feuds with his former friends – Tolstoy once even challenged him to a duel, and he wasn't the only one; and after a particularly acrimonious falling-out the poet Fet called him an extremely spoilt, unbridled egotist, unkindly quoting something an uncle of his had once said about him.

This quarrel, however, stands out from all the other spats and wrangles because it cut to the nub of something important and revealing about Turgenev. It doesn't matter who in reality shouted at whom, or who stayed calm and dignified. It doesn't even much matter whether or not Turgenev really did declare himself a German. What intrigues me to this day about this argument is the freedom to re-create himself as somebody else which Turgenev undoubtedly believed he had a right to. Like his good friend Gustave Flaubert (one of the few Frenchmen Turgenev actually liked), Turgenev took exception to the idea that one's 'fatherland' had to mean 'a certain piece of land traced out on a map and separated from others by a red or blue line'. I did, too, when I was young. But I didn't end up a Frenchman or a Russian – I just ended up globalised.

In a letter to his lover Louise Colet, Flaubert declared that for him his *patrie* or 'fatherland' was 'the land I love, that is to say, the one I see in my dreams, the one I feel at home in'. He went on cheekily: 'I am as much Chinese as French . . . [and] I love those fierce, enduring, hardy [Arabs], the last of the primitives, who stop at midday to lie down in the shade under the bellies of their camels and, while smoking their chibouks, poke fun at our great civilisation, which makes it quiver with rage . . .' Warming to his theme in a letter a couple of weeks later, Flaubert first hammers home his point that it's 'wildly stupid' to feel obliged to live in the red and blue part of the map and to hate the green and black parts of it, and then denies he belongs to any particular epoch ('I'm no more modern than ancient', he assures Louise Colet) or even to any particular species ('I am brother in God to everything that lives, to the giraffe and the crocodile as much as to man').

This was absurd, obviously – Flaubert was no more a giraffe or Ancient Greek than he was an Arab camel-driver, he was profoundly French – but it was *refreshingly* absurd. He was claiming the right to identify himself according to what he loved, rather than where he had been born, according to where his allegiances lay, rather than with a country that prided itself on its 'railways, poisons, cream tarts, royalty and the guillotine'.

WHATEVER TURGENEV ACTUALLY SAID to Dostoyevsky about Germany and being German, I like to think that he said it in the spirit of Flaubert's letters to Louise Colet. His disdain for Russia cannot be compared with Flaubert's for France – he'd never felt so bored, for example, by the sterility and banality of Russian life that he'd wanted to take a rifle and 'blow the heads off passers-by', as the young Flaubert had – but it's true that his primary allegiance was always to what he called 'civilisation', not to a country on a map.

There is a problem here, however. We can't identify only with what we love for the simple reason that we are already much more than what we love. Indeed, Flaubert's belief that we can and should hints at a mentality few Arab camel-drivers or Chinese, let alone crocodiles, would share.

Turgenev was profoundly Russian, obviously, not German at all. Even the way he conducted his altercation with Dostoyevsky strikes me as utterly Russian, unimaginable in the sedate world I live in. Every book he wrote (in his incomparably rich Russian) was rooted in

Russian landscapes, characters, obsessions and ways of thinking, from his *Hunter's Notes,* set in the countryside south of Moscow where he grew up, to his final supernatural tales.

For all that, I don't believe, as so many learned commentators seem to, that the fate of Russia was his main theme. As I see it, the fate of Russia was more the instrument on which he played his main themes. He was a *free* Russian, asserting his right to play whatever melodies he chose on his Russian violin.

———

When I'd told her something about this famous quarrel with Dostoyevsky as we dawdled in the street, Ilse, who is a Berliner to the core (I'm not sure how German she is), became eloquent on the subject of violins. There's an old German saying, she told me as we sauntered further along Schillerstrasse towards a much more interesting street at its end, about how it's not the violin that's important, but who is playing it – and what is being played. (There is in fact no such old saying, it turns out – she was making that bit up.) On her own Berlin violin Ilse has played (with great flair, I might add) Chilean and Mexican melodies, French solo partitas, one Egyptian interlude and a whole Greek symphony. It's one of the things I find so appealing about her. Flaubert would have thought her very civilised indeed.

Is my violin 'Australian' in any sense, I wondered aloud? Ilse made a quip about didgeridoos to avoid the question, but I wasn't having any of that. Certainly when I was a young man in the 1960s, about to set out on my great European adventure in search of civilisation, and perhaps even when I first met Ilse in Sri Lanka in the 1970s, I'd have denied that there could be any such thing. To echo Potugin's words from *Smoke* about Russia, I'd have been inclined in those days to mutter darkly about how my country 'owes civilised lands not just our sciences, our art and our laws, but even our sense of beauty and poetry . . . while our own so-called native . . . arts are trivial nonsense'. Everything of real value in Australian society, I'd have said then, as Potugin did about Russia, had been borrowed. The very notion of 'Russian art' makes Potugin laugh out loud – 'I've simply never come across any,' he says. (I *had* come across Patrick White by the mid-sixties, despite an education devoid of any Australian content, but White had after all been educated at Cheltenham College and Cambridge.) The only thing his country is good for is 'raw materials', Potugin says, the odd shipment of leather, bristle and tallow. In my experience, quite a few Europeans (although not Ilse, who has lived there) would say much the same thing about Australia today. For them Australia is still just a picturesque quarry. 'Tell me,' a well-read, educated Frenchman asked me recently in Paris, as one might innocently enquire about the state of affairs on some remote Pacific island, 'does culture exist in Australia?' ('*Ça existe en Australie, la culture?*')

I'd have been tempted, too, when I was young to agree with Potugin's thoughts about his native land, when he said it was peopled by 'slaves' – *holopy* in Russian, men born in and for servitude – not in any straightforward sense, of course, but in the more subtle sense that, as he puts it, 'We keep talking about our capacity for defiance as our great distinguishing quality. But we don't even defy whatever it might be like free men, swinging our swords, but like lackeys, hitting out with our fists, and we even do that at our masters' bidding.' (In Australia this kind of 'hitting out' is called 'larrikinism' or 'disrespect for authority'. It's the kind of futile ratbaggery which leaves authority yawning, a version of Dostoyevsky's 'raising hell'. In my view it's actually conservatism dressed up as rebellion for a bit of a laugh.)

However, I don't want to sound like a home-grown Potugin and bring the wrath of our home-grown Dostoyevskys down on my head. Besides, that was then, and I now see everything – Europe, civilisation, barbarism, Australia – in a rather different light. It's true that we are now but a distant satrapy of another great empire on the rampage, but this time around far fewer of us seem willing to be slaves.

IF YOU TURN RIGHT at the end of Turgenev's street and cross the river, you are in fact on Fremersbergstrasse. Just five minutes' walk up the hill would have brought us to Turgenev's villa, which he spent over three years building next door to the Viardots. (The architect, he maintained, was a scoundrel who had swindled him shamelessly.)

'Let's go there, then,' Ilse said, quite keyed up, I think, at the prospect of seeing something that was not just a plaque or figment of the imagination.

'Let's go tomorrow,' I said. 'Sunday's the day to go. It has to be Sunday.'

'Why?' Ilse likes to do things *now* – have dinner, read a book someone's mentioned, fly to Madagascar. By tomorrow we could all be dead.

'Tell you what,' I said, coming to a halt in the middle of the bridge across the Oos, 'I'll explain over lunch at Weber's.'

There is no Weber's, I knew that. Weber's is the name of the café next to the casino where Litvinov, reading the sensational news of Garibaldi's arrest over a dish of 'disgusting ice-cream', was first assailed by Potugin with his diatribe about all Russians being slaves. But there *is* the Kurhaus Bistro in much the same spot next to the casino entrance – the very spot where I had stood watching the polished display of Latin dancing the day before.

Sunday. Why Sunday? On Sunday mornings during those Baden-Baden years, at first in the pavilion behind the Viardot villa and then, when it was finally finished, in the theatre in his own mansion next door, Turgenev would take part in one of Pauline's 'musical matinées'. On any given Sunday, from the smart broughams and landaus lining the street outside might step Liszt, say, or Anton Rubinstein, director of the brand new St Petersburg Conservatorium; a famous artist or two, such as Gustave Doré – Pauline's husband was a serious art collector and had hung the walls of their pavilion with an impressive array of contemporary works; the Empress Eugénie, over from Paris to take the waters; Bismarck, the Duke and Duchess of Weimar, even Wilhelm, King of Prussia, and his wife Augusta, if they were in the vicinity; and an assortment of the *fine fleur* of European society, overjoyed at having secured an invitation to join this glittering assembly. Rubinstein might toss off a bagatelle on the magnificent concert grand or Pauline might even sing a few *Lieder* or play one of Schumann's fugues on the organ (with Turgenev pumping away on the bellows). Clara Schumann herself, one of Pauline's closest friends, would occasionally be present. She'd bought a house just outside Baden-Baden the year before the Viardots moved there from Paris and she and her close friend Brahms saw quite a lot of the Viardots (and Turgenev) during the summers they spent there.

How illuminating it would be to know what the two women talked about when they met. Both of them, after all, were married women with oddly childlike, complaisant husbands (although Clara's was dead by this time), both had been ardently loved by a young man of great beauty and extraordinary talent (Brahms and Turgenev). Both of them had sailed after many years into quieter harbours with their adoring erstwhile suitors in tow (not lovers but fixtures). Both were mothers of daughters their suitors also fell absurdly in love with. Both were sober, passionate, gifted, untouchable.

On the whole it seems to have been the assembly that was glittering rather than the music at these matinées, although the King of Prussia was impressed enough one Sunday morning to present Pauline with a bracelet as a token of his esteem. Out of delicacy, no doubt, he also gave her husband Louis a vase. As often as not, once the theatre at Turgenev's own villa next door was ready, the highlight of the morning would be a comic operetta with lyrics by the great Russian writer himself and music by Pauline Viardot. With their exotic settings in enchanted woods and harems, swarming with elves, magicians, pashas, Oriental princesses and black slaves, there were plenty of roles in these pieces for Pauline's students and children. Pauline herself, despite having moved to Baden-Baden because she was losing her voice, often took a leading role, while Turgenev would quickly switch from pumping the organ to outright buffoonery, throwing himself into the part of some freakish cannibal or wizard. Not everyone was amused. Even Turgenev seems to have wondered once or twice if this kind of undignified behaviour was quite appropriate. You didn't, after all, see Louis Viardot rolling around on the floor at his wife's feet dressed up in off-cuts from old curtains. 'I have to admit,' he wrote, 'that I shuddered when, lying on the floor in the role of the pasha, I looked up and saw a faint, contemptuous smile on the sealed lips of the crown princess.' But he always had a weakness for buffoonery. Who can forget the line from Tolstoy's diary: 'Turgenev. Cancan – sad.'

Needless to say, it was not only on Sundays that Turgenev visited the Viardots. Almost every afternoon, when he lived in Schillerstrasse, he would make his gouty way up the hill to the villa with its view over forested hills and meadows to see his friends, play with their children, or stroll in the gardens sloping down to the stream behind the house. When he eventually came to live next door, with his dog Pegasus at his side, he would even sometimes sneak into Pauline's studio during a lesson to watch the woman he loved teaching.

'Just make sure Pegasus doesn't start howling,' Pauline would say sharply and then turn back to the lesson at hand. She was a fierce teacher.

'I can't do it, Madame, it's beyond me, it's too hard.'

'Yes, you can. Try it again.'

'My voice just can't . . .'

'Yes, it can. Don't be so weak-willed. It's never easy. Now, try it again.'

And Pegasus would start moaning and Turgenev, smiling weakly, would reach down and hold the dog's mouth closed. Pegasus was by all accounts a superb gun-dog, well-known and liked around Baden-Baden. He had just one failing: he couldn't stand Pauline Viardot.

———

Ilse, I could see, was unimpressed by all the dukes and princesses, the pavilions and villas and Liszts and Schumanns, but curious about Turgenev's attachment to the Viardots. Although effortlessly at home in surroundings I sometimes find intimidating, she doesn't for an instant take any of it seriously. The emotions, on the other hand, she takes very seriously indeed.

'I don't understand,' she said, fork poised above the strudel. 'What sort of arrangement was this exactly?'

'I don't know,' I said. 'Nobody really knows.'

Ilse likes to know. 'I mean, were they lovers? What did the husband think? Or was it a *ménage à trois*? Did they all sleep in the same bed every second Tuesday? What was going on?'

I laughed – they were such *modern* questions. 'I think,' I said, 'he was more her troubadour, really, and she was his lady.'

'At his age?'

'Well, at the beginning, anyway.'

I could see that Ilse found this, not so much unlikely, as unimaginable. Such an arrangement is no doubt rare in Berlin these days. A complaisant husband, a wife with a sense of adventure (or the other way around) – this would have all been perfectly understandable, having a long history, especially amongst the leisured classes. Even a bisexual threesome would hardly have scandalised Ilse, I'm sure, if she'd run across one: the wealthy husband who adores his wife but likes yachting or the opera even more, especially in the company of a few well-turned-out young men. What a great catch, she'd no doubt have thought, for the woman who needs a touch of 'divine madness' from time to time (in Lou Andreas Salomé's phrase – and she knew what she was talking about) to keep conjugal happiness humming along. Ilse would have found this sort of thing as unexceptional as our own weekend together in Baden-Baden, itself an arrangement which the couple at the next table, I suspect, would have found at the very least outlandish. Troubadours were another matter entirely.

'Let's nose about the casino,' I said, changing the subject completely, 'when you've finished your strudel.'

'Nose about?'

'Exactly.' Ilse enjoys morsels like 'nose about'. 'How can we come to Baden-Baden and not visit the casino?' Half of Russia, after all – or at least half of a very thin, but glamorous, slice of Russia – had disgraced itself there.

'It will be wall-to-wall Arabs,' she said bluntly. She was far too curious, though, to let me go alone.

———

In the event we saw only one Arab. Most of the players in the public rooms we visited seemed to be what Dostoyevsky would presumably have called 'scum': perfectly ordinary people, the sort of people you see out shopping or walking the dog every day of the week. A little on the portly side, many of them, a little overfed, the women with a hint of gold on wrist and neck, most of the men fitted out in jackets and ties, looking like well-dressed bullfrogs, but not my idea of 'scum'.

The original chandeliers still hang from the ceilings, although not now candlelit, of course, the walls are covered in the same brilliant silks and hung with the original portraits (I seem to remember one of Madame Pompadour and another of the Empress Maria Theresa), the ceilings are still sumptuously frescoed, Chinese vases still stand where they once stood, and gold-tasselled lamps still hang low over the tables, just as they did in Dostoyevsky's day (and Hesse's, although he also mentions palms). It's Versailles, it's Fontainebleau, it's magnificent. It's also deeply dispiriting.

In *The Gambler* Dostoyevsky's narrator rants for pages about the 'squalor' and 'filth' of German gaming-rooms such as these. What could he have meant? In the Russian newspapers, he says, he was forever reading articles about the 'extraordinary magnificence and luxury of the gaming rooms' in the casinos on the Rhine. Yet what does he find? 'There is nothing magnificent about these squalid rooms . . . It all looked filthy to me – morally disgusting and filthy. I'm not talking at all about the greedy, anxious faces clustered around the tables in their dozens, even hundreds. I see absolutely nothing filthy in the desire to win as much as possible as quickly as possible.' No, what was ugly about the scene in the gaming-rooms was the 'respect of the gambling riff-raff for what they were doing, the deeply serious and even deferential way they gathered about the tables'. They trembled over a gulden. A true gentleman or lady, on the other hand, with footmen and flunkeys dancing attention, placed little piles of gold francs on red or black for fun, for amusement's sake, 'to observe the process of winning and losing'. What was squalid was not the décor, but the grim seriousness of the players.

At least in Dostoyevsky's day the décor matched the drama taking place around the tables. At least there were bluebloods and bankers losing fortunes in the blink of an eye, thieves and swindlers prowling from table to table, *lorettes* (high-class prostitutes, really) trawling for business, fights breaking out – in other words, ruin, corruption, despair and obscenity played out with a certain flair until the candles guttered. What was dispiriting the afternoon we visited was the absence of theatre – the stage-set was intact, but the play was over. We were left with the scene-shifters and cleaners. The faces around the green tables were blank, locked in a monklike trance. They were not even greedy and anxious. Our gamblers had the air of long-faced supplicants at a shrine. Perhaps that's what Dostoyevsky had meant by 'deeply serious and even deferential': ordinary people hoping in all seriousness for the extraordinary – a miracle.

'Hoping' is surely the key word here. 'Scenting fate,' Hesse calls it. Apart from the ennui, which no amount of dressing-up can disguise, it is above all hope you see fixed on the faces around the tables. I hadn't expected that. Dostoyevsky only hints at it once or twice, as far as I can recall, in *The Gambler*: 'However silly it may be, roulette is almost my only hope,' Polina Alexandrovna tells the narrator, who himself calls roulette his 'only way out and salvation'. Hope of what? The way out of what? Hope of riches, naturally, that goes without saying, and the happiness and freedom said to accompany wealth. But hope of something else as well, something it's hard to find the right words for without sounding overly metaphysical. Hope, I would say, for a blessing, for an event which would prove that there *is* a pattern to life after all, that escape (a 'way out') *is* possible, and that our lives need not be small, as meaningless as a mollusc's. If only we could break out of the cycle of circumstance, even momentarily, then anything might be possible – love, happiness, even God in some form, and also, in Hesse's phrase, an end to 'the cult of work'. Needless to say, Dostoyevsky's 'gentlemen' (who do not toil and whom he despises no less than the scum) already have all that sewn up. Dealt royal flushes at birth, they can afford to look on gambling as pure 'entertainment', splashing friedrichs d'or around for a bit of a laugh.

Turgenev gambled in Baden-Baden with the cards he'd been dealt, like anybody else, although not in casinos with the rabble. And, as Dostoyevsky had noted back in 1845, it wasn't a bad hand: wealth, talent, intelligence, even 'superb' good looks. 'Happiness' was what he was playing for, I presume – or at least *schastye*, as he'd have thought of it in Russian. This is a word with its roots in a syllable meaning 'lot' (as in 'lot in life' or, for that matter, 'lotto'), something rather more precarious, more in the hands of fate (or God, for the religious) than English 'happiness'. Happiness is not something you deserve or earn (like the dull Germans), but something that alights upon you. What Turgenev wagered was his immense capacity for love (in some sense of the word that is now flying apart, rather like a jigsaw the cat has slept on). 'Love is a bet,' Octavio Paz has written, 'a wild one, placed . . . on the freedom of the [beloved].' In Baden-Baden in the 1860s Turgenev placed all his bets on the chance that Pauline Viardot, finally, after twenty years of dilly-dallying, would freely choose to love him. And in her fashion she did, although not, of course, in the way he may have fantasised about as a young man, paying court in Pauline's dressing-room in St Petersburg.

EARLY ON THE SUNDAY MORNING, in brilliant sunshine, Ilse and I set out to visit the house on the hill which was the evidence of Turgenev's wager. On our way we had popped into the Trinkhalle near the casino to taste the spa water. For a few small coins you're given a plastic cup to hold under a tap. Its truly foul, acidic taste lingers in the mouth. We were wishing we could wash it away with a quick cup of coffee as we trudged up the steep hill towards Turgenev's house, but Fremersbergstrasse is villa territory, there are no corner shops or cafés in this neighbourhood. The street is lined with large, silent villas behind screens of pinetrees, birch and the odd magnolia. Discreet plaques announce the presence behind the shuttered windows of anaesthetists, specialised medical practitioners and therapists of all descriptions. The body is vitally important in Baden-Baden. Tending it as it falls apart is a hugely profitable enterprise.

There was nobody about. Occasionally a Mercedes-Benz would purr by, once or twice we heard a dog yapping, but otherwise we were alone on our walk up the hill in the sun. I'd been worried that there might be coach-loads of Russian tourists milling about as we drew closer – after all, they were milling about everywhere else in Baden-Baden: every café, ice-cream parlour and restaurant was crammed full of them, even the Trinkhalle had been swarming with Russians, all shouting '*Tfu! Kakaya gadost!*' in disgust as they tasted the spa water. But in Fremersbergstrasse we seemed to be alone. Not a Russian in sight. Perhaps in these post-Soviet times, unlike Turgenev on a Sunday morning, they were in church.

We almost walked past the house without noticing it. Suddenly Ilse's eye was caught by some scrolled gold lettering set into a wrought-iron gate: VILLA TURGENJEW. '*Ach du lieber Gott!*' she cried under her breath. 'This is it!'

I admit to a bolt of irrational excitement when I turned to look at the house. So he had stood *here*, he had walked through these very gates, he had . . . but was this the right house? This was not the noble Louis XIII manor it was supposed to be, with balustraded balcony and dormer windows in a slate roof. This was a rather messy, cream-coloured jumble of badly designed additions. In fact, it looked suspiciously like a rooming-house. We were just wondering what to make of it all when a young man drove up in a gleaming new sports car and parked right beside us. 'Can I help you?' he said in that irritatingly perfect English Germans affect. 'Looking for somebody?'

'As a matter of fact, we were looking for Turgenev's house,' I said. 'It says VILLA TURGENJEW on the gate here, but I don't think this is it.'

'No, the villa itself is up the road,' he said. 'These were the stables. You can come in with me, if you like, and have a look around. Not that there's anything to see, really.'

Ilse was striding up the side path before he'd finished speaking. And from the back of the house there was actually quite a lot to see, as it turned out. As I looked out over the sloping garden to the thicket of spruce and firs at the bottom and a line of green hills just visible in the distance through their branches, it was remarkably easy to imagine Turgenev making his way across the lawn, Pegasus at his side, to visit his friends next door – to rehearse one of their plays about wizards and elves in the pavilion; to talk to his *cher ami* Louis Viardot (now over sixty) about his translations of Russian writers or the hunting expedition they had planned for the next morning; perhaps (in his high-collared Russian blouse) to listen to some of the romances Pauline had been composing to the words of Russian poets; or he might simply have heard the boisterous shouts of the Viardot children and decided to go over and join in the fun. By now he was part of the family.

Where the rambling Viardot villa and pavilion once stood next door, there is now a modern block of apartments, stylishly angular in cream-painted concrete, with tiny balconies looking out on the forest of pines and firs – an elm or two, perhaps, as well, it was hard to be sure. Deep green. Very German. An anaesthetist, no doubt, behind every window. Verdi on the Bang & Olufsen. But not a trace of Pauline Viardot.

'The rumour is,' said the young man who seemed completely at home here, 'that Pauline used to slip across and meet Turgenev for . . . what is the word?' – well, the nice word is 'trysts', actually – 'here in his stables.'

Really? What rumour? I hadn't heard this rumour. I stared out at the garden and tried to picture Pauline Viardot, Europe's most famous mezzo-soprano and mother of four, picking her way through the flower-beds towards us for a roll in the hay with Russia's most famous novelist. I couldn't. I could quite vividly picture Turgenev crossing the garden towards the Viardots' mansion, but, try as I might, not Pauline coming towards us. It was not a matter of what did or did not happen – it was a matter of how I understood (or possibly misunderstood) what these two highly cultivated, passionate people from another time meant by 'love'. I think they probably meant by it something as distant from today's understanding of that word as *Eugene Onegin* is from Juvenal's *Satires* (so flamboyantly pagan they could have been written yesterday – Juvenal lived in times as out of joint as our own).

————

More and more by that Sunday morning I was coming around to the idea of Turgenev as a kind of troubadour – not even a love-struck knight, but a troubadour, a poet who offered his *fin' amors* (his refined love) as a service to his chosen (married) lady. Service was the whole point of courtly love, as I understand it: the vassal's offer of erotic service to his aristocratic mistress. The thought of the culminating act, that ecstatic burst of utter knowing, may have kept the troubadour's (and, for all I know, Turgenev's) flame burning, but the sustaining pleasure was in this burning flame – in the flowering of the erotic imagination, not in its sexual root.

For a wealthy Russian landowner like Turgenev there was no shortage of women ready to oblige with sexual relations (serf-girls, prostitutes, gold-diggers, bored wives). However, in neither his novels nor his life did Turgenev show much interest in complaisant women, despite the fact that his own daughter Paulinette was the result of one of these purely carnal encounters in his youth. For that matter, in neither his novels nor his life did he show much interest in copulation *tout court.* Overwhelmingly, what seems to have excited his erotic imagination was love freely offered, objects of desire insisting they were subjects. Whereas certain noblewomen in medieval Provence were able to play along with this fantasy, especially while their husbands were away at the crusades, few Russian ladies of quality in Turgenev's day could.

Twenty years earlier, Pauline Viardot, on the stage in St Petersburg and then in her castle at Courtavenel, attended by her pleasant middle-aged husband, must have seemed like the embodiment of the young Russian wandering minstrel's ideals. Here, though, on the hill above Baden-Baden, still acting out the vassal's role of service to his lady, he must have wondered on occasion if he'd been a fool to let one of life's great (if more prosaic) pleasures pass him by: family happiness.

Clearly there was much more to this story than medieval courtship. For a start, the attachment lasted for forty years, until the day he died. A troubadour's courtship was usually a much shorter-lived affair. There was also the influence on his emotions of his brutal, all-powerful mother to consider. With a mother like Varvara Petrovna, not to mention his distant, philandering father, who died when Ivan was sixteen, it's no wonder that his ideas about love were idiosyncratic, to say the least. Be that as it may, I couldn't see Madame Viardot picking her way through the grapevines and buddleias towards the stables at all.

———

'And is Turgenev well-known here in Baden-Baden?' I asked our friendly guide.

'Everybody knows the name, of course,' he said, as we made our way back up the path beside the house, 'but I don't think anybody much reads him nowadays. I'm actually trying to get a few people interested in putting on one of his plays here, just an amateur production.'

A Month in the Country, naturally. What else? He wrote it as a young man while staying with the Viardots at their castle at Courtavenel. A play about the old friend of the family in love with the wife. 'Enslaved, infected' by his love for the wife. A misunderstood embrace. A misplaced bet on the wife's freedom to love. (She actually uses her freedom to fall in love with her son's young tutor. Pauline Viardot, interestingly enough, used her freedom to fall in love with Charles Gounod, right under Turgenev's nose, although after the play had been written.) Love shattered. The end.

In the sun beside the path there were a few young men sitting around with newspapers, drinking coffee and chatting in a Sunday morning sort of way. Some of the other tenants, probably. Tanned skin, designer stubble. We nodded and Ilse said a few words to them in German. I wondered what they would make of *A Month in the Country*, if they ever got to see it: an aching, hopeless, unfulfilled love; enslavement 'to a petticoat'; educated adults, trailing about in an endless quandary, talking, talking, talking; nobody going to bed with anybody (apart from spouses, presumably). What, for that matter, would they make of the love affair that had unfolded all around them on this very path, in this very garden, nearly a century and a half earlier? Devotion, appetite, intimacy, yearning, with no final coupling on the horizon – all the elements in the plot would be familiar to them, presumably, but the plot itself would surely strike them as bizarre. They didn't look to me, with their sleek sunglasses and expensive haircuts, as if they'd be likely to spend twenty years in loving service to a mistress without bringing things to a head.

The villa, when we got to it a couple of doors up the hill, was uninviting, to say the least. VILLA TURGENJEW: KEIN ZUTRITT. No

ROBERT DESSAIX

entrance. I looked at it from across the street, I stood on my toes and looked at it over the hedge, I looked at it from the open gateway, and I peered through my zoom lens across the banks of roses into the sunlit, terraced garden falling away at the back. Imposing, severe, symmetrical. A bijou château. Perfect. And at that moment disappointingly closed off and lifeless.

Yet it was here where we stood, somewhere behind the windows of this French fantasy we were staring at, that my barbarian from Spasskoye, a miniature slave-state lying hundreds of miles south of Moscow, once ruled over by his appalling tyrant of a mother, had settled. He'd wanted 'simply to weave a little nest' for himself in which to 'await the onslaught of the inevitable end'. Just fifty years old, here he was at last, *grand seigneur* in his own little castle, nestled amongst the pines and firs on the most fashionable street of 'Europe's summer capital'. Here at last, in this small German town, halfway between Berlin and Paris, he must have felt definitively *civilisé*. (He liked to say it in French.) It didn't last long: two years after he moved into his little nest, the Franco-Prussian war broke out (you could hear the guns along the Rhine from Baden-Baden) and the idyll crumbled. He would have to 'await the onslaught of the inevitable end' elsewhere. (It's a mistake to wait for it anywhere, in my opinion. I like to keep moving.)

In a mad attempt to bring the villa to life, Ilse and I began prowling around beside and behind the house, trying to catch a glimpse through the trees of the garden at the rear. What we thought we were doing, I can't imagine. We found our way around the back of the flats next door. One of the residents spotted us poking about and flew out onto her balcony. 'Who are you? What do you want?' she called out. 'What are you looking for?' Not an easy question to answer. What, indeed? We retreated to the street.

58

Finding a little path down the other side of the villa, we circled around behind it through waste ground buzzing with insects. A few chairs and tables on terraces in a pool of sunshine, that's all we could see. Some wealthy industrialist's back yard. Well, what had we expected? Not, of course, the spectre of a long-dead Russian writer entertaining friends amongst the roses. And not a peek into the inner sanctum of a shrine, either, we weren't idolators. But what? Again, all we could see was an empty stage. All the scenery was in place, but the actors had long since gone home.

———

Many years earlier, in Europe for the first time in my life, I had seen the Berlin Wall. It had loomed up out of the fog near the Potsdamer Platz, as I remember, where you could climb onto a wooden platform and stare across the wounded landscape to the apartment houses in East Berlin. It had been not just a surreal experience, like time-travel or waking up with no warning in Timbuktu, but an implosion at the core of who I was. Everything had shattered in seconds: my concept of the East, of course, where my rose-coloured imagination had been rooted for ten years; my politics, my view of human nature; but, more dramatically, my smug sense of being whole. There on the Potsdamer Platz on that grey October morning I'd been forced to look at the very embodiment of the wall that cut through my own psyche. On the one side lay the modern city, chaos, pleasure, misery, humanity being utterly human; on the other side the ordered masses doing the bidding of their masters, paradise by decree. It had been an ecstatic, life-changing moment. But what has stayed with me across the years is one small sound: the screech of unseen streetcars, turning corners in the fog in East Berlin. That faint screech was the only reality we shared at that moment, the denizens of that grey paradise, an unbridgeable distance from where I stood (and also a stone's throw away), and I. It synchronised our separate realities. To this day, whenever I hear that screech of a turning tram – in Moscow or Melbourne, in Vienna or Helsinki – I implode again, just as I did on the Potsdamer Platz in 1965, in a burst of memories, arguments and anxieties. I am a child again, going to school on a Sydney tram. I am in Berlin. I am at the Bolshoi. I am in church singing hymns. I am cruising on the boulevard de Clichy, awash with libidinous fantasies. I am transparent. Just for an instant. Then I catch up with myself again. (It *was* just a tram.) Yet, having met up with myself again, I find I've changed. Just a smidgin, but I've changed.

In Fremersbergstrasse, on the hill in Baden-Baden, I think I'd hoped to catch the sound of something, like the screech of those Berlin trams, but it would have been a Turgenevan sound this time, something to remind me of who I once was and push me to reconfigure myself – just briefly, a tremor would have done, not a seismic shift. A snap refocusing on now. It didn't happen.

It's odd: the more perfect the stage-set, the less my imagination feels inclined to wander.

Back out on the street there was still not a soul about. We dawdled for a bit in the sun, taking photographs and admiring the late summer gardens. If it looked at all like this in Turgenev's day, no wonder he felt as a Russian that he'd arrived in the Garden of Eden. Russia was 'a disaster', he wrote to Pauline during a trip home the year his house was finished. 'I don't know if it's because of the famine they've just gone through, but I don't think I've ever seen such pitiful, ruined dwellings, such emaciated, sad faces . . . it's all grog shops and hopeless poverty.'

He even complained about the 'disgusting, filthy snow' blocking the streets. Russia was a 'prison', he wrote, with the tsar as head gaoler, despite the abolition of serfdom. And it was swarming with his enemies, too, right across the political spectrum: just about everyone, whether radical or conservative, had detested *Fathers and Sons*, and absolutely everyone had felt betrayed and insulted by *Smoke*.

YET EVEN IN BADEN-BADEN, it must be said, in this haven of beauty and calm, bathing in the warmth of Pauline's affection (which had been rekindled, there's no doubt about it, since they'd settled there, almost side by side), life was not all sweetness and light. On the contrary: it was during these years, his 'happiest', that Turgenev wrote his darkest stories. Anyone who has moved to ideal surroundings expecting bliss at last, as if time might stop, will understand. In paradise you always wake up one morning to the particular kind of spiritual desolation that lurks there and nowhere else. It has a quality all its own.

To those looking in at you from outside, your desolation (depression, melancholy, ennui, gloom, *taedium vitae, Weltschmerz* – there are dozens of words for it) will seem infuriatingly self-indulgent, naturally. When as a young man I first began encountering all the high-flown phrases in Turgenev's letters and other writings about the dark state of his ego at the age of fifty, his 'disgust with everything human' and the 'swiftly advancing shadows of death', I was less than sympathetic. Famous, rich, handsome, loved, living in luxury in one of

Europe's most beautiful towns – what more did he want? What did he mean by 'life's absurdity', 'life's futility' and 'the crackling sound of death . . . all around us'? Even on that Sunday morning in Fremersbergstrasse, I have to admit, standing with Ilse in front of his handsome château, its tiers of sunlit rose-beds glowing behind the house like the gardens of paradise, I felt a momentary Dostoyevskian crabbiness creeping over me.

Most puzzling of all to me when I was young was a sentence from a rather morbid piece of his called 'Enough', which he began writing when he first moved to Baden-Baden. 'What is terrifying,' he wrote, 'is that nothing is terrifying . . . Once you realise this, once you have tasted this wormwood, no honey will seem sweet to you.' Not even love.

———

Now, somewhat older than Turgenev was when he wrote these lines, living in my own antipodean Garden of Eden, at the very bottom of the world – in fact, the view from my windows over river and mountains is rather more beautiful than anything he could see from his villa in Fremersbergstrasse – I have a better understanding of his point of view. It's not that I'm particularly afraid of death, at least in the sense of the eternal nothingness which caused him such anguish, although, like him, I can distinctly hear its rustle 'all around us now'. No, what makes me warm to him and want to re-read him with more sympathetic attention is a glimmer of fellow feeling – I think I now know what that wormwood tastes like. Depression, fear, even panic – all those things are to be expected, obviously, from time to time in the course of anyone's life. And it's not a simple matter of unhappiness, either – like Turgenev in Baden-Baden, I am almost disgracefully happy. It's a matter of having tasted the wormwood. It's a taste no honey can sweeten.

In the strange (frankly, almost unreadable) fantasy called 'Apparitions', which he was working on when he moved to Baden-Baden, he puts his finger quite deftly on where this taste comes from. One of his kinder critics called it 'a capriccio with a Hoffmanesque taste to it', but most readers took a deep dislike to 'Apparitions'. This is not surprising: a brooding narrator, borne aloft by a vampire with the ludicrous name of Ellis, is regaled with a series of 'dissolving views' or 'apparitions': the first is of a shipwreck off the Isle of Wight, where Nature wipes out a multitude of insignificant human lives with her usual indifference; the second is of the devastation wrought by humans themselves on other humans – the Roman legions in the Pontine Marshes; the third is of another mass murder of human beings – this time by the rebel Stenka Razin on the rampage on the Volga; the fourth is of Paris, the very pinnacle of civilisation, which strikes the narrator floating above it as a raucous, decadent, ugly, doomed 'human anthill'.

Given his itinerary, not to mention the blood-sucking, it's no wonder the levitating narrator was overcome by a 'feeling of revulsion, and even more strongly and more than anything else . . . a feeling of revulsion for myself'. Perfectly understandable. A glance at any newspaper can have a similar effect.

This revulsion is not the nub of the matter, however. The other feeling these 'dissolving views' aroused in the narrator – and this is what I did not understand when I first read 'Apparitions' as a young man – was tedium, a sense of the banality of what we are experiencing. What he saw did not so much terrify him as make him feel numb. We now see it on television every night, up close and in vivid colour, no need for a vampire: 'a powerless population crushed by misery and sickness and chained to a lump of despised dust . . . more insignificant than flies . . . their comical battling with what cannot be either changed or avoided . . . everything'. Both nature and humanity, from this perspective, are unfeeling and doomed to extinction. To contemplate further the pointlessness of life on this 'fiery grain of sand which is our planet' becomes merely wearying rather than horrifying. This is the wormwood whose taste we cannot forget.

Turgenev's way of living with this bitter taste in his mouth – and it must be lived with – was through resignation, an acceptance of his own impotence in the face of the forces that rule our lives: fate, blind chance and the implacable laws of nature. He found some comfort in loving and being loved, although in middle-age he probably felt he'd reached the *dénouement* in the tragi-comedy of his life – quite literally the 'unravelling' of all those strands (lust, friendship, sentiment, adoration, loyalty, hope) which when we're young are woven together to form the cord called 'love'. He was certainly beginning to feel that he had missed out on 'the main prize in life's lottery', by which he meant, I take it, his own nest in some conventional sense – twenty years of playing the troubadour was no doubt taking its toll. It is, after all, a young man's game.

There was always the comfort of art, of course, although he was conscious of how depressingly momentary everything we create is, even Shakespeare's plays or Beethoven's symphonies, and how vulnerable to the mockery of the crowd. His friend Flaubert took a more cavalier approach: to hell with the mob, the 'love of art' was 'everything' for him. His pleasure in transforming the world, in other words, outweighed the world itself. 'I worry more about a line of verse than about any man', he told Louise Colet, to whom this was presumably not wholly welcome news, 'and . . . I'm more grateful to the poets than to saints and heroes.' Thousands dying for their country in some Roman war or other, for example, were of little consequence according to Flaubert, compared, say, to Horace getting the iambics right in his poem about 'the little Persian boy Pollion has let you have'. It's a point of view.

Given his spiritual desolation, his joylessness (unrelated, as I see it, to unhappiness) and given his comfortable circumstances, I find it odd that Turgenev did not drift into mysticism of some kind. Inner emptiness and a full stomach, after all, make a good start. He did dabble in the supernatural, but that is not the same thing at all. Some trigger was missing in his psyche, something failed to fire. He made an effort from time to time to put his spirit in order, as one does at a certain age, but putting your spirit in order best follows some sort of insight, surely. No transforming insights were granted him.

But that sounds prim. It's not for me to judge how Turgenev dealt with his anguish. We must each of us deal with our anguish as best as we can.

Riding in the funicular later that afternoon through the firs and pines to the top of the Merkurberg, I took pleasure once more, as I always do in her company, in Ilse's effortless ability to make life good and revel in it. How does she do it? I can never quite work it out. Certainly not through resignation – Ilse is not resigned to anything. Yet she by no means closes her eyes to the things that chilled Turgenev's soul – she grew up in Berlin during the war, after all; until recently she worked in an old people's home, listening to the 'crackling sound of death' on a daily basis; she has seen what nature and humanity are capable of, from Phnom Penh to the football stadium in Santiago. She, too, I think, although much loved, has failed to win what Turgenev thought of as 'the main prize in life's lottery' (a mere spouse doesn't qualify). And she has no religious faith at all, as far as I can see, or even much sense of its absence. Yet she is joyful. I almost turned to ask her how she did it in the funicular car, but didn't. And once we got to the top, as happens on the top of mountains, it didn't seem important any more to find the words.

All of a sudden, as we stepped from the car, we experienced that 'delightful horror', as Edmund Burke called it, which vast panoramas afford. You are at once God and nothing. Simultaneously you are the sky and a grain of sand. Far below lay the Black Forest, a string of brilliant green valleys, the toylike town of Baden-Baden and, away to the west, a sliver of the Rhine and France. It was all so much gentler than what I see from mountaintops at home, but still the sense of a void – of nothingness breathing on you and leaving a blank space where you once stood – was thrilling.

And right in front of us, as we left the funicular station, people were leaping off the edge of the summit into this nothingness. A few seconds after each figure hurtled off into the sky, a parachute would snap open in a burst of colour – red, yellow, green, purple: the sky was alive with swooping half-moons in glowing colours. We stood transfixed, watching them first soar up into the blue and then slowly begin to eddy downwards. It was sublime.

Eddy downwards.

All of a sudden – a dull rattle, a change in the light – I was coming down to earth myself. I was crossing a bridge over a yellowy-brown river. '*Meine Damen und Herren, in wenigen Minuten erreichen wir Strasbourg.*' The Rhine – that must have been the Rhine. No border controls these days, I could have been anywhere. 'Ladies and gentlemen, next stop: Strasbourg.' Huge blocks of flats, factories, fly-overs. '*Mesdames et messieurs . . .*' A cavernous railway station. Boss again – no, Calvin Klein. We screeched to a halt. It was bedlam on the platform outside. Loudspeakers booming, crowds surging – talk about 'anthills'! I sat tight. The compartment filled up with Serbs and Sri Lankans. Nobody seemed to be speaking French. I got a whiff of potato crisps and watery coffee.

Just four more hours and I'd be in Paris.

PART TWO

FRANCE

———

'I languish when from you, and am wounded when I see you, and yet am eternally Courting my Pain.'

CHARMANTE IN APHRA BEHN'S *EMPEROR OF THE MOON*

PARIS

HIGH UP ON THE WALL of number 50 *bis*, rue de Douai, in Paris – so high up you need binoculars to read it – is another plaque:

> **Ici vécut de 1871 à 1883 l'écrivain russe**
> **IVAN TOURGUÉNIEV**
> **auprès de ses amis**
> **Louis VIARDOT, historien d'art et hispaniste**
> **et Pauline VIARDOT-GARCÍA**
> **cantatrice et compositeur**
> **sœur de la MALIBRAN**
>
> *(Here from 1871 to 1883 lived the Russian writer IVAN*
> *TURGENEV close by his friends Louis VIARDOT, art historian*
> *and Hispanic scholar, and Pauline VIARDOT-GARCÍA, singer*
> *and composer, sister of LA MALIBRAN)*

Nobody expects a plaque to tell the unvarnished truth, some diplomacy is to be expected, but this is little short of mealy-mouthed.

After leaving Baden-Baden together with the Viardots, Turgenev took several rooms on the third floor of this unremarkable building on the edge of Montmartre, directly above the Viardot family apartment on the second. It was his 'home' (he loved to use the English word) for the last twelve years of his life. But he didn't live simply 'close by' (*auprès de*) Louis Viardot and his wife, and certainly not in that order, and the Viardots were by no means simply his 'friends'.

It's true that the gentleman in Turgenev would probably have approved of that '*auprès de*', especially on a public plaque, but to my mind it is far too cautious, too respectful an expression, having echoes of such phrases as '*l'ambassadeur de France auprès du Vatican*'. In the rue de Douai, Turgenev and the Viardots were a trio, a functioning threesome.

It's also true that he did call Pauline Viardot his 'friend' – *amie, Freundin* – but what other word was there? In the letters he wrote to her whenever he was away travelling at this time he often addressed her (in German) as 'most precious friend', but in these same letters he was also apt to sign off (also in German) by kissing her 'dear, magnificent hands for hours on end'. This '*theuerest Freundin*' business strikes me as a chivalrous mask, concealing the profoundest intimacy. If she was a 'friend' by the time they all moved to Paris, she was an *infinitely* loved friend. By 'infinitely loved' I mean that, like two mirrors face to face, they reflected each other into infinity. Or else, as he wrote revealingly right at the end, she was his *only* friend.

Pauline for her part, later in life, called Ivan Sergeyevich 'my heart's choice' – a pregnant phrase if ever there were one.

He also addressed her husband, Louis, as '*mon cher ami*', but then he called almost everybody '*mon cher ami*' in his letters, so it's hard to gauge what weight to give the expression. Perhaps the older husband his infinitely beloved came with was indeed best described as a 'dear friend'. Perhaps there is no other word for the accommodating husband of one's beloved. Tom Stoppard in his recent epic drama about nineteenth-century Russian radicals, *The Coast of Utopia*, has one of his Russian characters dismiss poor Louis as 'the postillion', but this is unnecessarily cruel. All three of them were in the coach.

———

Paris is, of course, plastered with plaques. What we are supposed to do with the information these plaques impart is anybody's guess. Perhaps knowing that a famous painter lived here or an illustrious writer died there (Zola was in fact asphyxiated just around the corner at 21 rue de Bruxelles) spurs passers-by to reflect on their own place (or lack of it) in the pageant of history.

Questioning, presumably, the whole notion of a pageant, some wag is going around Paris as I write, putting up plaques commemorating nothing. *Karima Bentiffa, civil servant, lived in this building from 1984 to 1989*, one such plaque reads in the rue Saint-Sauveur, for example. *Here on April 17, 1967, nothing happened*, announces another. And, in a stab at distilling the absurdity of the whole plaque enterprise – possibly of the idea of significance of any kind – he's even put up one which says: *This plaque was put up on December 19, 1953*. This sort of playfulness is dangerous: it suggests that the lives of the great and good are as devoid of meaning as ours are. Or that the lives you or I are presently leading are just as meaningful as the lives of the great and good. I'm surprised the authorities haven't had it stamped out.

In general I quite like plaques, I must admit – they can give you a sense of perspective. In the small city in Tasmania where I now live, plaques are few and far between, as the great and good have been. Important things have happened here, obviously, but not anything of importance to anybody of importance. Recently, for instance, on a pretty cottage in a side-street on the edge of the town centre, I noticed a plaque which, after telling me that the house was classified by the National Trust, simply reads: *Malolo Cottage, circa 1850.* No mention of anyone from the pages of history being born there or of any literary masterpiece being created there, no hint of any prime ministers, Olympic heroes or movie stars having once slept there.

All the same, as if I'd been stood on my head for no reason at all, everything suddenly looked different when I read that National Trust plaque: it was all still solidly there, of course, but turned around or given a fourth dimension. Everything – the house, the cars, the trees in the park at the foot of the hill. Upside-down, I studied the neat little pumpkin-coloured house in front of me for a moment or two, then drifted down the hill towards the park, my head abuzz with thoughts about what sort of people might once have lived in a cottage like this, and what it must have felt like *circa 1850* to be living in a god-forsaken settlement in the south-east corner of Van Diemen's Land. At that time Hobart Town was just a scattering of houses and public buildings on the Derwent estuary, a dangerous voyage of six or eight months under sail from England, closer to the South Pole than to civilisation. In 1850 it was still swarming with brutalised convicts, too, some newly arrived, some doomed to the lash or noose. In those days it was still hemmed in by forests and mountain ranges teeming with outlandish plants and animals, as well as the ghosts of stone-age men and women. (Except on the sunniest days, over a caffelatte in one of the tarted-up warehouses down by the docks, some would say it still is.)

All this less than forty years before my father was born a thousand miles to the north. As a young man my own father must have actually come across people who had walked down this very hill, past these very stones, when this town was just a dusty speck on the map of Van Diemen's Land – 'too close to the rim of the earth', as Abel Tasman had written gloomily, sailing away, 'to be inhabited by anything but freaks and monsters'. In the blink of an eye, as if zapped by that little plaque, I felt I'd turned into a bridge between that land of monsters at the end of the world and the crowds of leisured coffee-drinkers lounging in their designer clothes from Milan and New York at tables outside the chic cafés and delis beyond the park. (In fact, if I'd taken off my glasses and squinted, I could have imagined I was in an antipodean Leopoldsplatz by the sea.) Five months under sail to England? If I'd wanted to, I could have jumped into a taxi to the airport, flashed a credit card and been in London before sunrise the next morning.

Abruptly I was the right side up again, a bridge to nowhere. Van Diemen's Land crumpled into a tiny paper ball, flew off behind me on the wind and disappeared.

———

'Would you like to see the fabulous Beckmann exhibition at the Centre Pompidou?' It's the sort of thing everyone asks you in Paris before you even have time to unpack your suitcase. That you're starved for culture is taken for granted. 'What about the homage to Roland Barthes?' Also at the Centre Pompidou, as it happens. (I don't think so.) 'Jackie Kennedy's clothes and accessories?' Just the White House years, apparently, not the whole kit and caboodle. That's at the Musée de la Mode et du Textile. (*Non ça . . . je pense pas!*) 'What about the Frankfurt Ballet tonight? How often does a company like *that* visit Tasmania?' (Not often.) But I say no to all of them. First off, the thing to do in Paris is walk. It's the walking and looking and listening and smelling you'll remember for the rest of your life.

In all the years I've been visiting Paris, for example, I've only been to the Louvre once – and can scarcely remember a thing about it, except for the crowd of Japanese blocking my view of the *Mona Lisa*. What I do vividly remember, however, is crossing the forecourt of the Louvre late one chilly evening, heading for the river, and turning to see the rumbling city beyond the black of the Tuileries Gardens glowing red and gold and white like an approaching lava flow. And in its path, oblivious to the threat, there was a giant ferris-wheel, turning slowly, ablaze with orange lights. Snatches of music on the wind, too. And I thought: 'The Metropolis!' – that's the precise word that came into my head. A menacing word which makes you want to flee back to the steppes and forests, and at the same time an unbearably exciting word which makes you want to stay where you are forever. In a similar vein, I hardly remember the view from the top of the Eiffel Tower, but do clearly recall eavesdropping on the conversation of some Australian tourists in the ticket line at the bottom. And exactly what I saw inside the church of St Germain des Prés escapes me, while the smell of *crêpes à la crème de marron* in the street outside, where I've strolled many times just watching the passing crowds, still lingers in my nostrils.

So in Paris I like to walk, trying out the rich array of French verbs I know for drifting along on foot: *flâner*, of course, with its hint of idleness; *se promener*, more purposeful, a little livelier; or I might feel inclined to *me balader, baguenauder, déambuler, musarder, errer, faire un petit tour* – there's no end to this flurry of French walking verbs and I've tried out every one of them in Paris.

———

I'm not sure exactly which one I was enjoying the afternoon I came across that plaque in the rue de Douai, but probably my favourite: *déambuler.* I was mooching about on foot. Although it's just a stone's throw from the garish boulevard de Clichy and the Moulin Rouge, where I usually take a stroll for old times' sake, the rue de Douai belongs to a different world entirely. I doubt it's changed much since the Viardots, with Turgenev in tow, established their town residence there on the corner of the rue de Bruxelles, when it was still quite new. Lined on both sides with elegant five- or six-storey neo-classical apartment blocks, with tall Palladian windows, some shuttered, and those massive wooden entrance doors the French have a liking for, it seemed tranquil, indeed almost suburban, the afternoon I found it. Schoolchildren were loping along the footpaths in gabbling groups, delivery men were delivering, blocking the street with their vans as usual, dogs were busy everywhere I looked (Parisian dogs are always very busy), while in the tiny chestnut-shaded Square Berlioz on the corner opposite Turgenev's windows – a remnant of the old Tivoli Gardens – mothers sat with prams and children squealed in the sand-pit. Instead of the present modest statue of Hector Berlioz, it was once briefly possible to admire a statue of Napoleon here, completely nude. Rudely defaced soon after it was erected in 1850, it had to be hastily removed.

Standing outside the *boulangerie* beneath Turgenev's windows, breathing in the smell of freshly baked bread, I could see both the

Sacré Cœur, a bluish smudge against the colourless sky to the north, and a toylike Eiffel Tower in the south. (Needless to say, neither of them was there in Turgenev's day.) However, apart from these landmarks, and the cars and vans jamming the street, I imagined that what I was seeing was pretty much what he saw when he left the house for a stroll, to meet up with friends or to carry out some task for the Viardots – his Russian guests were sometimes flabbergasted to find that the great writer had been sent out like a servant on some errand for his mistress. Pauline, for her part, was indignant about the stream of 'barbarians' from the steppes clambering up and down her polished Paris staircase.

On a fine winter's afternoon, if you'd been passing, you might have seen him pottering off in the direction of the Tuileries, less to read than to sit on a bench and watch the world go by, much as he'd once done on his beloved Lichtentaler Allee in Baden-Baden. In a sense, this mournful, gravelly expanse (I've never quite grasped its charm) was his old stamping ground because, before moving to Baden-Baden, he had lived with his daughter right opposite the old Tuileries Palace Gardens, halfway along that dazzling colonnaded stretch of sheer elegance called the rue de Rivoli. A little run-down nowadays, with its bric-à-brac shops and beggars, it was still quite new in the 1860s and rather smart.

Predictably, there's a small plaque attached to the wall next to the massive doors of number 210, announcing with solemn inaccuracy that Ivan Tourguéniev lived there from 1860 to 1864 and wrote *Fathers and Sons* there. (He actually moved from here to Baden-Baden with his daughter in 1863 and wrote only about half of *Fathers and Sons* in Paris.)

The morning I last passed that way none of the blasé foreign tourists sitting at the tables outside *Le Welcome* café a few metres away or browsing through the postcard stands in front of the shop next door showed any sign of noticing the plaque was even there, let alone of caring who this Tourguéniev character might be. 'Don't you realise,' I felt tempted to call out to the group of young English-speakers lounging over cokes and cakes at *Le Welcome*, 'that a book written upstairs in this very building changed the course of Russian literature? As a matter of fact, *your predicament today* is described in *Fathers and Sons* with incomparable sharpness of vision, poetry and truth. You should get yourselves a copy.' To be fair, they probably hadn't noticed that they were in a predicament. Or if they had, they probably thought it had something to do with terrorism. (And I'm quite sure they wouldn't have caught me out quoting Isaiah Berlin.)

Your real predicament, I'd have said if any of the gaily clad young tourists had wanted to know, the one which this Russian writer sat down to describe in the winter of 1860 in a room above where you're now sitting, is what happens when 'the soul', as we used to call it, begins to evaporate, as it did in certain radical circles in Russia in the late 1850s. At this point I'd very likely have lost most of them – the word 'soul' has that effect on people nowadays, except at funerals. They'd probably have written me off as just another loony – the streets of Paris are full of middle-aged men who have veered off the rails.

If I'd persevered, though, I'd have liked to ask them if they could even imagine what it would be like to live in a world where they naturally thought of their fellow human beings as 'souls' rather than as clusters of molecules, two-legged orchestras made up of billions of minuscule mechanical pianos. Our predicament, according to the author of *Fathers and Sons* – everyone's, I'd have emphasised, not just yours – is not that everything is therefore permitted, as Dostoyevsky thought, but that love is therefore almost impossible. If they'd stared at me in disbelief – after all, love is probably what they thought they were connoisseurs of – I'd have begun to stumble. You can enjoy the music, you see, I might have continued, but can't love in any meaningful sense a host of miniature pianolas, even if it has a face at the top. And if you can't love, this Russian who lived above you would have said, there's no point in staying alive.

Of course, if any of them had actually bought a copy of *Fathers and Sons* and read it, they'd almost certainly have been mystified by my summary of its main theme. Isaiah Berlin would have been appalled by it. After all, molecules and pianolas are never mentioned. They'd have taken it to be a book about the angry gulf between Russia's youthful free-thinkers and their fathers' generation in the mid-nineteenth century, or the death of the Romantic era, or the birth of modern revolutionary ideology – and they'd have been right, up to a point. These are indeed the shards making up Turgenev's mosaic. Bazarov, the atheistic young medical student at the novel's centre, represents all those things. If you stand back, though, and consider the mosaic as a whole, I think (as always in Turgenev's novels) a different picture emerges. Since the middle of the nineteenth century, when the soul was put on notice, it's been extraordinarily difficult to love.

ON CERTAIN SUNDAY AFTERNOONS in the 1870s in the rue de Douai, on your way home from the *boulangerie* with a sweet-smelling baguette under your arm, you'd have glimpsed Turgenev setting off to pay Flaubert a visit in the rue du Faubourg St Honoré where he kept a flat. In fact, a year or so after his friend moved to Paris, Flaubert told him in a letter that 'if you weren't living in Paris, I'd give up my flat . . . straight away. The hope of seeing you there occasionally is my only reason for keeping it on.' Zola would sometimes turn up at these get-togethers as well, along with Alphonse Daudet, Maxime du Camp and one or two other writers. I can just hear them railing in their cutting French way about the 'irredeemable barbarism rising from the bowels of the earth', as Flaubert put it in a fit of *Weltschmerz* in 1872, 'the hatred for everything great nowadays . . . the disdain for beauty, the execration of literature.' At least, Turgenev might have mused, the French had once had a civilisation for the barbarians to overrun – and knew it.

Just before midday was the moment to catch Turgenev heading off for breakfast. He was partial to breakfasting late in a café somewhere down towards the Opera with friends and confrères – not quite as late as his friend George Sand, who liked to breakfast around four, but certainly not before noon. By noon he was awake enough to enjoy vigorous conversation, although not yet ready to write – not that he ever wrote very much in the rue de Douai, preferring to write at his summer house at Bougival outside Paris or during his frequent trips back to Russia.

Rebecca West has claimed that 'there is no such thing as conversation. It is an illusion. There are intersecting monologues, that's all.' Too often true, as we know, but it was not true at all of those midday breakfast conversations, if his friends' reports are to be believed. Henry James, for example, wrote that he always left these breakfasts 'in a state of "intimate" excitement . . . the condition in which a man swings his cane as he walks, leaps lightly over gutters, and then stops, for no reason at all, to look, with an air of being struck, into a shop window where he sees nothing.' (He makes it sounds suspiciously like falling in love.) When Turgenev talked, according to James, he 'vivified' his companion's imagination, whatever the subject of the conversation and whether or not you agreed with him. What a gift!

Most afternoons and evenings, however, you'd have waited in vain for the tall figure with silver hair and beard to emerge from number 50. In his slightly cramped and shabby drawing-room upstairs, with its vast divan and green, cloth-covered walls hung with fashionable paintings (Millais, Théodore Rousseau, one Corot – he liked a nice landscape), he would almost certainly have been playing host to a stream of guests. The cream of French literary society regularly made its way up the Viardots' staircase – Zola, Daudet, the Goncourts, Mérimée, even Flaubert on occasion – but so did a multitudinous mixed bag of 'barbarians from the steppes': Russian writers, intellectuals, revolutionaries, pilgrims and any number of young men wanting to borrow money, Ivan Sergeyevich being such an extraordinarily soft touch. On one occasion he even entertained God and his prophet, an unusual twosome from anyone's point of view: touring Europe looking for converts, they'd dropped in just on the off-chance to sound out the possibilities at 50 rue de Douai. They were wasting their time with Turgenev, of course, who had no more interest in God than in cricket, but no doubt they were received with disarming courtesy.

If he did happen to find himself at home alone, he had the joy, if he was so minded, of picking up the special speaking tube he'd had installed and listening to his beloved Pauline giving her singing lessons in the room below. Her voice was going, but for Turgenev there was no sweeter sound.

———

Despite this appearance of endless conviviality, Turgenev did not actually much like the French. Or so he claimed. On the whole, he once said, he found them 'cold, petty and banal'. 'It's hard for me to live in France,' he once complained to a Russian friend, 'where poetry is petty and miserable, the natural scenery is positively ugly, music is reduced to vaudeville or a joke – and the shooting is disgusting.' Not even the literary luminaries he knew well could win him over – George Sand, for example, he found too 'garrulous', Lamartine was 'a whiner' and Mérimée 'disgustingly obscene'. For the most part he preferred the company of visiting Russians – and there were hordes of them in the French capital by this time, Paris in the seventies being 'in' and Berlin 'out' with the Russian smart set. He also had his own little clutch of Russian expatriates he liked to mix with.

There's really nothing unusual about that sort of preference: in Bolivia or Bhutan we all like to bond with the 'natives', naturally, steering well clear of anyone from home, but when we arrive in any of the great metropolises, especially if we're from the fringes of civilisation, we regularly seek out our fellow-countrymen for company. We antipodeans, for instance, start ringing around from the airport within minutes of clearing customs: friends, friends of friends, even somebody who once met a friend of a friend – they're all potentially part of our defence against organised foreignness on such an intimidating scale.

However, when Turgenev wrote in 1857 (to Tolstoy) that he hadn't met a single attractive woman in Paris, apart from a certain Russian princess, or a single intelligent man, apart from one German 'Yid', one begins to suspect that it was less the French that he detested than his own situation in France, living out of the spotlight, uprooted, far from the land he drew his inspiration from. Perhaps, too, like the Goths arriving in Rome, he felt that curious need of the barbarian to sack – to 'trash', as we might say colloquially nowadays – what he had dreamt of possessing all his life.

Not that Turgenev was ever personally a barbarian – on the contrary, he spoke three languages faultlessly and a number of others well, he was a connoisseur in literature and music, he was well-travelled, urbane, and possessed the kind of knowledge of history without which taste is impossible. He was just highly conscious of belonging to a tribe the French, including the Viardots, regarded as barbarian.

Turgenev wasn't as rude about Paris as some of the other Russians who flocked there. A kind of servile detestation of all things Parisian was almost *de rigueur* amongst members of the Russian intelligentsia (not unlike the servile detestation of all things American amongst

Australian intellectuals today): the historian Karamzin, for instance, remarked on the city's 'superficial splendour', Gogol attacked its 'superficial glitter, concealing an abyss of fraud and greed', Prince Vyazemsky, one of Pushkin's friends, wrote dismissively about the 'deception and falsity' of French society, Herzen called Paris 'Europe's spittoon', while Tolstoy more excitedly, if unoriginally, came up with 'Sodom and Gomorrah'.

This conviction that, whatever was wrong with Russia, it had something precious which other countries lacked – 'soul', perhaps? – was alive and well even in the Soviet era. I remember a Soviet guest in Canberra in the 1960s, still reeling from her first visit to an Australian supermarket, saying to me with all the hauteur she could muster: 'Yes, you have everything, but we are *morally* superior.' You merely *have*, in other words, whereas we *are*. At that point in my life, never having tasted Soviet life for myself, I half thought she might be right.

———

Turgenev, too, claimed that he 'loathed' Paris, like his illustrious fellow-countrymen, complaining about its 'formal sameness'. What could he have meant by that? After all, in the rue de Douai, on the edge of Montmartre, he was living just a short walk from the elegant *quartier* which Balzac a couple of decades earlier had called the capital's 'palpitating heart' (between the rue de la Chaussée d'Antin and the rue du Faubourg-Montmartre, not far from the Opera House). 'Once you've set foot here,' Balzac went on, 'if you have any imagination, you can give up on the rest of the day. It's a golden dream, irresistibly distracting. You're at once alone and accompanied.'

Rhapsodising over the engravings, prints and books, the mouth-watering delicacies and confections of diamonds on display in the shop windows, the latest shows in the cabarets and theatres and the throng of alluring women sauntering along the streets, Balzac declared it all 'so intoxicating' and 'so exciting' that by rights the police should forbid the poor even to pass that way.

By the time Turgenev settled in the rue de Douai, right on the edge of this 'palpitating heart', Balzac's Paris, of course, had been transformed by Haussmann. The *grands boulevards* had sliced straight through the cluster of medieval villages which made up Paris in Balzac's day, the first department stores were opening their doors to the bourgeoisie, cafés were turning into brasseries and the streets he'd have passed along on his way to the Opera or the restaurants he frequented would have appeared even more opulent, even more ostentatiously middle-class than on his first visits to Paris. Yet he remained unmoved. He was an aristocrat, not a stock-broker, property not trade, and he did not find this kind of display of middle-class extravagance appealing – and indeed found the middle-class characters in Balzac's novels who did 'nauseating'. Feudal and dilapidated Russia might be, but at least it was not middle-class. I wouldn't be surprised if he probably also hankered after the messy spaciousness of Russian towns and villages. After a few days in Paris I usually find myself hankering after something similar. It's a mystery to Parisians.

He was unlikely to find the scene at the end of his street to his taste, either. This was the sort of neighbourhood which quite appeals to me – every now and again, just for a lark. Just round the corner from the rue de Douai, merging into Montmartre, was an area the Parisian bourgeoisie had long visited '*pour s'encanailler*', as the French so picturesquely put it – 'to slum it', we might say, 'to mix with the rabble' – an area of dance-halls, taverns and brasseries frequented by petty criminals and ladies of easy virtue who at certain times of the day poured out of the side-streets onto the main thoroughfares like flocks of partridges (in Balzac's phrase – and he was a hunter).

———

It wasn't all scum, though. In the neighbouring rue des Martyrs, for instance, at the very time Turgenev was in residence a few blocks away, the famous Brasserie des Martyrs was in its heyday. According to his friend Alphonse Daudet, during those very years the Brasserie des Martyrs was a 'literary powerhouse' – just being one of its regulars made you famous, he said. Every evening 'between eighty and a hundred *bons garçons*' would gather there

> to smoke their pipes and empty their tankards. People
> called them bohemians, which didn't bother them at all . . .
> You should have seen the place in the evening, towards
> eleven, enveloped in a hubbub of voices and the smoke
> from all the pipes! . . . Anyone of importance had his own
> table which would become the kernel, the centre of a whole
> clan of admirers . . . Here's the thinkers' table . . . and here
> they are, bareheaded, beards cascading down, surrounded
> by the smell of coarse tobacco and cabbage soup and
> philosophy. Further over are the jackets and berets and all
> the yelping, caricatures and puns. They're the artists,
> sculptors and painters . . . The beer-glasses keep coming,
> the waiters are dashing about, the discussions heating up.
> There are shouts, raised arms and tossed manes of hair.

Not quite Turgenev's scene, clearly (he preferred drawing-room conversations or gatherings in chic restaurants like Magny's), but it is evidence of an animated artistic life not far from his front door. Indeed, as my modern guidebook euphemistically suggests, this area has 'lost nothing of its animation' even today.

It was pretty 'animated', for that matter, I noticed, at the other, closer end of the rue de Douai, just two blocks away to the west. Above the milling crowds from the four corners of the earth, illuminated advertising hoardings in front of the Pathé multiplex cinema on the Place de Clichy blocked the end of the street with gigantic, lurid images of lust and death. (And something about that corner suddenly rang a little bell.)

WHATEVER THE ROOT REASONS for his disparaging attitude to France, by the time he moved into the house in the rue de Douai in 1871 he had managed to spend a large part of his life in the country. By 1871, of course, the gallant young knight at the castle gates in Courtavenel was playing the part of much-loved member of the family, doting on the children, going hunting with the chatelaine's amiable, if rather stuffy, ageing husband and coming downstairs on Sundays to take part in a game of charades.

As in the case of Brahms and Clara Schumann, however much Ivan Sergeyevich kept bemoaning his lack of a 'nest', something about an attachment to a married woman actually suited him down to the ground. It saved him, as it did Brahms, from any possibility that his love would degenerate into a routine exchange of banalities or become swamped by all the vulgar duties in which marriage (even for the rich) abounds. Nests may be cosy, but they're also banal and messy.

All the same, wherever he looked, he saw people in pairs. A young troubadour at heart he may have been, but it's tempting to feel bereft in middle age if you're not one of a pair. 'Get married,' he told his young friend Anatoly Koni, visiting him in Paris from St Petersburg, 'it's essential to get married. You have no idea how painful a lonely old age can be, when you're forced to take shelter on the edge of somebody else's nest, to accept kindnesses like charity and be in the position of an old dog which isn't chased away only out of habit and pity.'

Notwithstanding this *cri de cœur* dressed up as advice, nothing in his fiction points to any inclination at all, at any point in his life, to imagine married coupledom as the setting in which a great love might flower. A hedge against loneliness it might well be, but marriage is nowhere depicted in his works as love's white-hot brazier. Without exception all his main characters die, commit suicide or have the curtain abruptly rung down on them before married bliss can take root. It was love he was enamoured of, not marriage, but love freely given.

He may never have read the writings of Eleanor of Aquitaine's daughter, Countess Marie, who presided over the Court of Love in twelfth-century Champagne, but the general tenor of her judgements would have struck a bell with him, I'm sure. 'We declare and hold it as firmly established,' she wrote bossily in 1174, 'that love cannot exert its powers between two people who are married to each other.' An expert, like her mother, in the refinements of courtly love as practised in the north of France, she claimed that this judgement was 'supported by the opinion of many great ladies . . . [and] should be to you an indubitable and eternal truth.'

———

Interestingly enough, the Countess Marie and her husband Henri (whose opinion on these matters is not recorded) often held court, surrounded by up-and-coming troubadours, at Provins, just over the horizon from the castle at Courtavenel.

Her judgement may have been a trifle harsh for Turgenev's taste, if he ever read it. He may have felt more affinity for the line taken by Andreas Capellanus a decade later in his *Art of Courtly Love,* a sort of troubadour's bible. While admitting that marriage is 'no excuse for not loving', Capellanus suggests that ardent love for one's legal spouse is little short of perverted – in fact, practically *adulterous*, in his terms, because it is a betrayal of love itself. The triangle for Capellanus, in other words, was made up not of the shadowy husband, the lady and the troubadour, but the lady, the troubadour and love, which they both served. (Peasant women, he declared – Turgenev would have winced at this point – should not be instructed in love because it would distract them from their labours. If you wished nonetheless to copulate with such a creature, and came upon a convenient place in which to do so, you should not hesitate 'to take what you want by force'.)

Be that as it may, in the rue de Douai, approaching sixty, Turgenev pined for a nest. Some might say that a 'nest' is precisely what he had in Paris and Bougival, and had had in Baden-Baden, even if of an unconventional kind. Strictly speaking, the fledglings may not have been his (despite the rumours to the contrary), but they may as well have been. His feelings for Claudie and Marianne Viardot in particular (he thought the son an 'ill-mannered boor' and a drunkard) were always much warmer than his feelings for his own daughter.

Despite his being part of the Viardot family, many of his own visitors at number 50 rue de Douai were less than impressed by his circumstances.

The same Anatoly Koni, a well-heeled St Petersburg jurist, was shocked by the blinds which had come adrift from their moorings in the living-room, the dust on the furniture, the disorder in his small bedroom, the missing buttons on his coat. The subtext here is indignation at the Viardots' neglect of Turgenev's welfare. Quite why they should have been responsible for cleaning his flat and sewing on his buttons is a mystery. Obviously a man of his means and stature could not be expected to attend to these matters himself, but he could easily have paid somebody else to take care of them.

Even Henry James, a staunch admirer of Turgenev's with no particular barrow to push, found his circumstances 'dingy' and the Viardots 'a rather poor lot'. 'To live with them,' he said with an audacity the Viardots would not have appreciated, particularly in an American, 'is not living like a gentleman.' The youthful James doubtless found the Thursday and Sunday parties *chez Viardot*, at which the great Russian novelist was given to capering about embarrassingly on all fours dressed up in bizarre costumes, both outlandish and demeaning to the man he so revered. He certainly found them tedious: 'they were musical,' he wrote, 'and to me therefore rigidly boresome.'

Their own relationship worked much better when he and Turgenev met in restaurants.

———

The question of nests aside, was Turgenev happy in the rue de Douai? A fatuous thing to wonder, some might say – 'happiness', after all, means such different things to different people. Nevertheless, standing on the corner across from Turgenev's windows, on the point of drifting on, I couldn't help mulling it over.

Did the man who once lived behind those windows really feel (as he'd claimed in Baden-Baden) that at root his wager on happiness thirty-odd years earlier had been squandered? Is that what 'missing out on the main prize in life's lottery' had meant? His first love for Pauline had been 'extinguished' by her (and this was her word, not his) years before, snuffed out like a naked flame before it could set the whole house ablaze, but by the time he settled in his flat in Paris a second love for her, if not exactly incandescent, was burning steadily. He had happiness of a kind, surely, although not, perhaps, of the kind celebrated in most romances and comedies.

Intriguingly, just as he was moving into this house in the late autumn of 1871, he was putting the finishing touches to one of his most charming, richly autumnal stories about happiness, *Torrents of Spring*. The hero, Sanin, a young Russian landowner at a loose end in Frankfurt, is presented with two extreme options – the same two, as it happens, being canvassed in glorious colour at the Pathé multiplex cinema at the end of the rue de Douai on the afternoon of my visit: firstly, the Christian option (the man saved from dissolution by pairing off in marriage with a virtuous, beautiful woman); and, secondly, its devilish counterpart (dalliance with an alluring, wanton adventuress, leading to a life of dissolution). True to form, the Turgenevan hero, making a hash of both options, slips sullenly into that shadowy, unsung space between them. (As many of us tend to do, some with more grace than others.)

To be completely frank, I think it was quite a good outcome in Sanin's case, given the choices. He behaved rather caddishly towards the virtuous beauty, I agree, after promising her marriage and eternal love, but, when all was said and done, he was a Russian nobleman and she was just a pretty nineteen-year-old Italian girl, daughter of an immigrant pastrycook. The second option, a lifetime spent as a voluptuary's plaything, was even more of a delusion. One night, one week, one whole summer at the outside – but a lifetime? A frolic in the woods while the wanton's husband turned a blind eye might be put down to a lust for experience. Following her to Paris, where he was dumped, was a mistake.

Sanin falls in love with the pastrycook's daughter, Gemma, in the blink of an eye in her father's backstreet *Konditerei*. When you're twenty-two, this sort of thing happens all the time, especially in summer in foreign parts. A dollop of sentiment is mixed with lust, fizzes up like a sherbet and is declared to be 'love'. It's for precisely this kind of effervescence that we go abroad at twenty-two. It's ravishing.

Since Gemma is already betrothed to a German businessman, Sanin needs to do more than sing pretty songs around the pastrycook's piano, however, if an urgent bolt of lust is to become a traditional folktale with a proper beginning, middle and ending, which is what bourgeois Italian parents in 1840 expected a bolt of lust directed at their daughter to become.

Sanin's solution is to start rescuing people: he rescues Gemma's younger brother from a fainting fit; challenges a drunken soldier who has insulted his inamorata to a duel; rescues her from her engagement to the (predictably) starchy, arrogant German; and eventually promises to rescue her whole family from poverty by selling his estate back in Russia and refurbishing their *Konditerei* on the proceeds. Her mother is already enthusiastically redesigning the shop's shelving when the wanton, a voluptuous Russian called Maria Polozova, appears on the scene and the whole thing falls apart: our knight in shining armour is revealed as an impostor, his gallantry a mere ploy. In any case, in my experience, people tend not to love their rescuers with any lasting feeling, although they may suffer a few twinges of gratitude for a while and, indeed, like Irina Ratmirova, offer the odd moment of *quid pro quo*. Late in life Turgenev himself wrote that almost any feeling at all can grow into love, even hate, fear and contempt – except one: gratitude. 'Gratitude is a debt you owe,' he wrote, 'but love isn't money.' It's those they rescue, those who are in debt to them, that people tend to love – unforgivingly.

It's during a little excursion to Wiesbaden that Sanin is ensnared by Maria Polozova, who is married, conveniently enough, to an infinitely understanding husband. ('I don't interfere in my wife's affairs.' 'You don't? None of them?' 'No, none, my friend. She goes her way . . . and, well, I go mine.' This was heady stuff for Turgenev's readers in the 1870s.) To amuse herself Maria seduces Sanin while out horse-riding with him in a nearby forest, 'enslaves' him and whisks him off to Paris to join a herd of other young male playthings. In abandoning Gemma, however, he soon finds himself abandoned in his turn by the voracious Maria and lurches into that plotless space between the two time-honoured storylines. For all this, although he turns into a bored and embittered bachelor, disgusted with life and terrified of death, he at least does not end up selling cakes and boiled lollies in a Frankfurt pastry shop for the rest of his life. The only glimmer of happiness on the horizon – just a throwaway line at the end of the novel – is in the extraordinary idea he suddenly comes up with in his mid-fifties of moving to New York, where Gemma turns out to be living happily, and no doubt virtuously, with her husband and children, to perch adoringly on the edge of her nest. *Torrents of Spring* is actually a moving story, masterfully told, but fortunately it ends here.

As he put the finishing touches to it, in the flat across the street from me on the rue de Douai, I imagine that Turgenev, too, had given up any hope of living out either of the two great happiness narratives, which still fill our screens and the pages of our books: a loving two-some on the one hand, endless debauchery on the other. Misery is rumoured to fill the gulf between these two celebrated storylines. Does this mean that he felt that on the whole his wager on happiness had not paid off?

Once upon a time, adrift on my own strict notions of what happiness was, I might have thought he had good reason to feel this. Now I tend to think that by the time he took up residence in the rue de Douai in his mid-fifties, it is more likely that he had simply given up trying to picture a happiness different from the one he was enjoying. People do. It's not a matter of never grieving over the world around you – of never tasting the wormwood in your mouth. It's not a matter, either, of never imagining being swept off your feet by somebody else (the man next door, Nicole Kidman – it could be anyone), of never having intoxicating night thoughts or even the odd adventure. It's more a matter of simply recognising that the web of loving relationships you have presently come to rest in will probably constitute the core of your happiness for the rest of your life. Not every blissful moment in your life will spring from it, presumably, nor every illumination find its source in it, but it will be your happiness – and your sadness and anguish as well, no doubt, but then happiness (unlike joy or bliss) encompasses those things.

For Americans happiness is not a question of wagering anything, of course, it's a matter of lawful pursuit. Their Declaration of Independence guarantees all Americans the 'unalienable Right' to pursue 'Happiness' as if it were a brace of snipe. For the rest of us, I suspect, and particularly for Russians with their notions of *schastye*, happiness is less a quarry than a chance configuration of circumstances we try to make the most of. We bet our freedom on it in marriages, our marriages on it in affairs, our livelihoods on it in casinos. I think that the handsome, silver-haired man in his mid-fifties who once came and went through the door across the street from me, for all his grumbling, would have had to admit to himself, if pressed, that his wager had, on the whole, paid off. Certainly it had not left him empty-handed.

If Turgenev *was* at times unhappy, I tend to think nowadays, it was more because he was practically friendless in the world than because he missed out on family happiness. It may seem an odd thing to say about such a companionable man who was on friendly terms with anyone who was anyone from the Atlantic to the Urals, but, for a man with little aptitude for nesting with a wife and children, he strikes me as strangely bereft of truly intimate friendships. There was Flaubert, it's true, and Belinsky, his adored mentor when he was young, whom I think he did love in a Russian sort of way not encouraged in the society I live in. However, Belinsky died when Turgenev was only thirty. There was nobody in his life, as far as I can see, he could lovingly wound and be wounded by, nobody he could wake up in the morning feeling harpooned with joy at the prospect of seeing that day. Once he'd fallen in love with Viardot, everyone else appears to have played the part of supernumerary in the drama of his life, fading back into the wings as he followed his diva across the stage. An intimate friend is never out of the spotlight.

For all his charm, it must be remembered, there seems to have been something about Turgenev which made friendship with men in particular difficult. Direct as usual, Tolstoy once called him '*kakoi-to zadira nepriyatny*' – 'an unpleasant trouble-maker' – *zadira* having bullying overtones. His good looks and habit of begging to be spoilt may have won many female hearts, but with men he could obviously become fractious and few lasted the course as his close friends.

From my perspective, however, at a similar point in my own life, there was actually an element of courage in Turgenev's acceptance of his unfitness for conventional domestic bliss – in his being reconciled to living as good a life as he could in the unplotted space between family happiness at the one extreme and unbridled licentiousness at the other. To live a *good* life there, rather than just mouldering away in dank self-pity, as Sanin did, takes both courage and imagination.

Turgenev no doubt had more of both of these qualities than Sanin – more, perhaps, than most of us, although he'd have denied it – yet the astonishing common judgement on him, as well as on his heroes, is that they were 'weak'. In a similar vein, Flaubert, followed by the entire Viardot clan, took to calling his friend 'the soft pear' – affectionately, but not unpointedly.

It's true that he shilly-shallied constantly – he was hopeless at dealing with time, he was always late, everyone mentions it, because he just let time unfold of its own accord. It's true, too, that, like almost all his heroes, he could be infuriatingly indecisive when called upon to act, but you *would* be hopeless at making decisions about anything pivotal in your life if you'd had a mother like Varvara Petrovna. As pitiless, absolute ruler of her fiefdom south of Moscow, she made sure that all decisions of consequence, especially regarding money matters, remained in her hands alone, taunting her sons with their powerlessness until the day she died – which she did in 1850, when Ivan was thirty-two years old, leaving, as he put it, 'the multitude of lives which depended on her out on the street'. The first mistress to enslave Ivan, in other words, was his mother, and for the rest of his life he was attracted to 'strong' women who were able to forge real lives for themselves.

Yet, if placing his fate in another's hands came naturally to him, that didn't mean he was 'weak'. It fitted him (and quite a few of his fictional heroes) out nicely for the role of wandering minstrel, singing, until virtually the day he died, of the hopelessness of his love, the freshness of his despair and his perverted joy in being denied what he most longed for. This was a song, though, not a confession of weakness. Even all-powerful emirs in medieval Spain sang it. 'Men are weak, women strong and chance all-powerful,' he sings in *Smoke*, but it was no truer on his lips than on the emirs'. Chance is obviously not all-powerful – that is the whole point of falling in love: the will seizes on what chance has delivered into its hands, turning a coincidence into something that was 'meant to be'. A man who can love a woman steadfastly for a whole lifetime, in the face of rejection, impossible distances, universal disapproval and her own rock-solid marriage, may be a fool, but he is not weak.

———

Unplotted though it is by most of our film-makers and novelists, it's in the ill-lit space between family happiness and unfettered depravity that most of us, surely, also spend our own lives lurching fitfully about. I have little doubt that most of the Parisians sitting around the patch of fake grass in the Square Berlioz while I planned my next move were in fact stuck there – the mothers with prams, the old men with faded eyes peering at their newspapers, the smartly dressed young men and women striding past with briefcases, even the chattering teenagers streaming home from school along the rue de Douai. It was hard to believe that, for any of us, a Hollywood romance was on the cards, let alone a pornographic extravaganza. All of us, except for the school-children, looked vaguely tired of ourselves, as if we'd run out of ideas about how to be different from who we were.

Still, sooner or later, we'd all have to go back to a room or a flat somewhere, close the door behind us and set about reinventing love and happiness, pleasure and plot, according to our lights. It would not be easy.

ALL OF A SUDDEN, just up the street from where I was dawdling, a little red and white train trundled across my field of vision, packed with middle-aged couples in tank-tops and sneakers. I squeaked across the polystyrene lawn to the corner and up the rue de Bruxelles past the Viardots' side windows towards where this completely different world was spinning. It began practically next door to the Viardots' with the Eva Kabaret bar ('PRIVATE SHOW TABLE DANCE') – what would Pauline have thought, I wondered, if she'd clapped eyes on an establishment like that just round the corner from her front door? Next came the Café Oz Australian Bar (words which would have been almost meaningless to the Viardots in the 1870s). And then I was there, on the Place Blanche.

It was like stepping out of a garden-party straight into a circus-tent: lights flashing, music throbbing, badly dressed crowds milling about and the smell of cheap food and vomit everywhere. I stood across from the Moulin Rouge for a moment, slightly dazed, and then sauntered off along the boulevard de Clichy towards Pigalle. What Turgenev might have made of it all I wasn't sure, but I admit I was a little shocked.

101

A vast sexorama, peep-shows, porno cinemas, erotic supermarkets, shop windows overflowing with sex videos, sex dolls, sexy underwear, leather and latex contraptions for every orifice, as well as a sleazy pinball parlour or two, a tattoo artist's squalid studio, and (*naturellement*) McDonald's. On and on they stretched, into the traffic-choked distance, these tawdry temples to the orgasm, each more garish than the one before. '*Du jamais vu! Toutes spécialités!*' Never seen before – really? *All* special tastes catered for?

The passers-by that afternoon seemed strangely oblivious to these blandishments. Perhaps to them they were all just part of the scenery nowadays, something that passed across their field of vision on the way to pick up some tomatoes at Monoprix, like clouds or the dome of the Sacré Cœur. Would it be a friskier crowd after dark? On the other hand, compared to what they were hurrying home to download from the internet, perhaps these live sex shows and shop windows full of whips and leather gadgets struck them as little more than quaint. Their faces gave nothing away.

In the grand scheme of things, I don't suppose these temples to the orgasm are much tawdrier than the run-of-the-mill temples to the body that cram the far more salubrious streets hidden behind the multi-storeyed Sexorama. These latter establishments are less directly focused on the genitals, obviously, but still, it had been bodies every step of the way from the Opera to the rue de Douai. Every single store and boutique along the way, it had seemed to me, every office, studio and hoarding, catered exclusively to tending the body: bistros, brasseries and delicatessens; pharmacists, herbalists, hairdressers and homeopaths; dress shops, shoe shops, tanning studios and travel agencies enticing you inside with images of lithe, young bodies at play in the sun. It was only marginally more edifying, when you came to think about it, than what *Souvenirs sexy* on the boulevard de Clichy had to offer. It wasn't so much *what* these businesses were offering that was off-putting – we all need to eat and clothe ourselves, after all, and there's nothing wrong with an orgasm in itself – rather it was the high seriousness of this public dedication to the body. Dostoyevsky's rant about the 'deeply serious and even deferential way' the gambling riff-raff gathered around the tables in the Rhine casinos popped into my head. A blueblood of the spirit played differently.

I'd seen enough. Even the Jesus and Mary in the window of St Rita's chapel across from the Moulin Rouge had seemed tainted by their surroundings – erotic in a grave, high-minded sort of way, about as spiritual as the inflatable dolls in the window a few doors up the street. I made for the metro station at Place de Clichy.

In the train – with an infinitely sexier ambience, from my point of view, than anything I'd seen on the boulevard de Clichy – I contemplated the astounding, half-naked form of a young African man swinging from a strap at the end of the carriage (loose-limbed and honed to perfection) and asked myself what, if anything, would scandalise that true blueblood of the spirit, Turgenev, if he could pop back to his old neighbourhood for an hour or two and take in the sights. Yes, his writerly eye rarely strayed in any focused way below the neck; yes, he always lowered the curtain before any carnal passions were actually played out. But I doubt very much that anything he'd see at the Pathé multiplex or along the boulevard behind his old house would strike him as a scandal in itself.

Debauchery, after all, was an honoured tradition in France long before Ivan Sergeyevich's time, a common way of playing at being somebody – anybody – else for an hour or two, of taking a little holiday from whoever you felt trapped into being. (Even today what is shocking to the French about the porn star Ovidie, who likes to quote Heraclitus, Simone de Beauvoir and even Bakunin in publicly defending her chosen profession, is not the acts she performs on screen but the fact that she's a vegetarian.) So nothing the 'Sex Posse' might get up to in Cinema 3, or anything that might happen at the 'Slave Auction' in Cinema 4, for that matter, would be likely to strike Turgenev as unheard-of lewdness.

What would shock him if he could join me now, I decided, observing the way the young African man at the end of the carriage was chewing gum with his mouth open and stroking his left nipple, was the way that acts that he had thought of as private were now being committed in public. What would appal him, I rather thought, was the way creating sexual cravings was now big business, as insatiable as the appetites it was whetting. Maria Polozova may have inflamed Sanin's passions, but she did it in private, with feeling, for her own amusement, not as a business venture. She was as free as 'a free Cossack', she boasted, and saw no reason not to take advantage of her freedom as she chose. What would depress Turgenev, surely, was the failure of the erotic imagination, not the panoply of lusts; the confusion of the erotic, which is all imagination, with purely physical sensation. And the cold salaciousness of what advertised itself as hot.

Then again, my troubadour might not feel shocked or appalled at all by what he saw. Before vanishing back to the late nineteenth century, he might simply dismiss the whole scene as hideously 'poshlo', a deadly mixture in Russian of the vulgar, the coarse and the mindless, and wonder why those with more refined sensibilities should be forced to look at it. What had happened since his day, he would probably wonder, to turn the purely sexual into the main arena in which to experience the self?

I would draw the line between private and public at a different point from Turgenev, obviously, or even from my mother, but also at a different point from where my friends' children draw it, not to mention the silky-skinned young African man at the end of the carriage. He had just dropped adroitly into the now empty seat beside his girlfriend and was devouring her like a ripe fruit. (At least he seemed to be feeling something.) I let my eyes fall back onto the newspaper article I'd been reading about a massacre in the Middle East. I am also inured to the public display of the sex industry's wares, even in middle-class environments, as Turgenev was not. At the same time, as I imagine he would have been, I am aware of the fading from view, under this onslaught, of something beautiful and important in the way we experience ourselves.

IT WAS THEN THAT IT STRUCK ME. By a strange coincidence, it had been on the Place de Clichy, on the very corner of the rue de Douai right in front of the Lycée Jules Ferry, just a hop, step and a jump from Turgenev's front door, that many years before I had embarked on my first sexual adventure. No wonder this corner had rung a little bell.

Although, like Sanin, I was in my early twenties then, adrift in a lively foreign city (it was in fact my first evening in Europe), I was not, as it happens, bowled over by a vision of beauty I wanted to pounce on and ravish, as he was; nor did I for a moment confuse my pleasurable agitation with 'love' of any kind, as he did – I was of my time. I knew exactly what was possible when the fair-haired young man about my own age loitering a few feet away – Roger his name was, it sounds much more elegant in French than English – asked me with a smile if he could help me decipher the map I was perusing. (My first night in Paris, streets going off at all angles, nothing meaning anything to me except 'Pigalle' – I needed that map.) Feeling that twinge of sweet anguish I suppose we all feel when somebody eyes us with a mind to our sexual possibilities, I let him lead me along the boulevard de Clichy, dazed by the explosion of colour and swaggering bodies, to a mirrored café blue with cigarette smoke, crowded with black-eyed Moroccans . . . and eventually (I can't remember any tentative 'Will we? Won't we?') he drove me back to my dingy hotel in the Latin Quarter, followed me upstairs (under the cold eye of the receptionist) to my tiny, yellow room high up under the roof and, without much finesse, got down to business.

The whole thing was a huge disappointment to me, to be honest. For that matter, I was probably a huge disappointment to Roger – after all, I was hardly an inventive partner. By the same token, my curiosity had been aroused, and, although I went on to live out, almost to the letter, Sanin's dream of marriage to a virtuous beauty – except that her father was no pastrycook – I remained actively curious about whether what happened with Roger in the little yellow room in the Latin Quarter need be all there is if you decided to go off in that direction.

In retrospect, that encounter with Roger from Rouen on the corner of Turgenev's street all those years ago was my first inept attempt to reconnoitre the space between family happiness and debauchery. The terrain is actually vast, once you get inside it, which can be difficult because there's a considerable log-jam of ditherers and gawking tourists at the entrance. For quite a few years I loitered there with the mob, gawking, myself. Now at home there, I inhabit it differently from Turgenev, naturally, with far less sense of resignation and far greater peace of mind. All the same, we'd have much more in common, I now think, if we were to meet up in some time-warp, than I would once have expected.

———

Back in my hotel room (speaking of time-warps), I found a note pushed under my door to ring Daniel. *Pourquoi pas?* I was in the mood by this time for some good talk, preferably with someone with a sense of adventure. And a car. After all, you couldn't get to Courtavenel without one.

Daniel thought lunch the next day sounded perfect.

COURTAVENEL

'WHY EXACTLY WOULD YOU WANT to go to see something that isn't there?' Daniel asked.

He did have a point. I'd just finished explaining to him over a deliciously crunchy *sandwich jambon* (the coffee was dishwater) that there was nothing left to see at Courtavenel, and now here I was trying to talk him into driving me there. Daniel, I might say, was still in his Buddhist phase that summer, so, strictly speaking, if I'd correctly understood the thrust of his Himalayan guru's teachings, he wasn't *completely* there himself. But I decided to let that pass.

'Ah, well,' I said, 'that's what I'd like to find out, you see.'

'What would you like to find out?' Daniel wasn't being difficult, he was quite simply curious.

'Well, I'd like to find out what, if anything, happens – of course, nothing at all might happen – when you go to a place where so many things have occurred, things you know about, things you've imagined vividly, and just stand and look.'

He nodded thoughtfully and swallowed another spoonful of his leek soup. I've always admired that mixture of intensity and utter calm in Daniel. Then he said: 'Are you expecting spirits? *Des fantômes?*'

We'd met in Kuala Lumpur, of all places, a few years before, when he'd been in his Sufic phase. He'd asked me to take his photograph in the butterfly house at Lake Gardens – we'd had to wait for a trembling, iridescent blue creature to alight on his shoulder – then we'd run into each other again in one of those crowded, aromatic streets around Bukit Bintang and had a meal together under a sign which read: REFLEXOLOGY CLINIC. IN DOOR AND OUT DOOR. FOR THE HEALTHY FOOT. Those are the kinds of trivial things one remembers about pivotal moments. What we actually talked about now escapes me. Sufism, butterflies, Baudrillard, tie-dyeing – with Daniel it could have been absolutely anything. He had a moderate interest in everything. The only forbidden topic was the Louvre, where he did something mysterious with computers.

In Kuala Lumpur he'd had a head of tight, black curls, but in Paris he was looking more monastic. His shaven skull was bent over his soup. He was thinking as he sipped.

'Where exactly is this Courtavenel?' he said, with the smallest of smiles.

'It's near a town called Rozay-en-Brie,' I said. 'East. In Brie. Not far. An hour or two away at the most.'

'Flat as a pancake, the country around there,' he said, reaching for some bread. 'Funny place to have a castle.'

In a way it was. Whenever I'd pictured the castle at Courtavenel, I'd pictured it (pennants flying from the turrets, drawbridge down) in proper castle country with crags, ravines, forbidding forests – that sort of thing. But as we got closer to Rozay-en-Brie that afternoon – we'd left straight after lunch ('*Okay, let's do it,*' he'd said in English, '*let's hit the road*') – the countryside stretched out in every direction as flat and featureless as Kansas. Or as most of my own country, for that matter. The sky that day was completely Australian: a dome of flawless blue enamel, scoured by the rains the night before.

We'd got lost, as one always does, trying to get out of Paris. A single wrong turn on one of those roundabouts, a moment's hesitation as you zoom towards one of those spaghetti-like tangles of fly-overs and off-ramps, and you find yourself careering off to Nogent-sur-Marne instead of Chennevières-sur-Marne or some other triple-barrelled town with 'Marne' in its name, and, before you can turn around, you're caught in a traffic-jam, staring crabbily at a Pizza Hut for half an hour. Or a brand new housing estate, used-car yard, petrol station, hyper-market, high-tension powerline, Buffalo Grill . . . Even Daniel got a little snappish and began correcting my French.

Then, at the wave of some wand, it all disappeared. Emptiness. Soothing expanses of maize and barley ready for harvesting, patches of forest and here and there a farmhouse. Far away on the horizon a church steeple or two. In Rozay-en-Brie, a few streets of sleepy shops and a jumble of pinched houses, some half-timbered, above a river, we made some enquiries of passers-by about Courtavenel. There seemed to be no signs to it and it wasn't marked on our map.

'Are you sure it was Rozay-en-Brie it was near and not some other en-Brie?' Daniel asked after a lot of blank smiles and puzzled looks. 'There are lots of them.'

'Of course I'm sure,' I said. 'It's where they all caught the coach to Paris. The castle was a stone's throw away from here, practically within walking distance. I'm amazed nobody has heard of it. The Viardots, Turgenev, Gounod, Berlioz, Charles Dickens . . .'

'Charles Dickens came to Courtavenel?'

'Half of Europe did, it was a mecca. It was a huge castle with a moat. How can these people never have heard of it?'

'Well, you said there was nothing there.'

'There must be *something*,' I said. 'A brick, an old gate-post, a cherry-tree, *something*.'

Eventually a blind man watching a wedding at the town hall told us to go on to Pécy, a few kilometres further east, and ask there. Now the land was really flat, like a breadboard strewn with a few clumps of greenery. What on earth had possessed the toast of Europe to buy a castle way out here on this plain of beetroots and barley, a long day's bumpy ride in the early 1840s in a diligence from Paris? Why not on the Loire or over towards Dijon, which is where the Viardots supposedly came from?

Then, away on the horizon ahead of us, as we came out of a patch of beech, we caught sight of Pécy, a few black scratches and squiggles etched against the blue.

'He wasn't a hunter, this Viardot fellow, was he?' Daniel asked. 'See all these signs to watch out for deer? I'll bet he wanted to hunt.'

He certainly did. Like his friend Turgenev, Louis Viardot was a passionate killer of wild birds and animals. All his life, both in France and Germany, he roamed the forests with his dogs slaughtering the wildlife. Nothing gave this studious, withdrawn and kindly man more pleasure than killing living creatures. As lord of quite a vast domain here at Courtavenel, spreading out from his medieval *château* across fields and forests teeming with wild boar, roe deer, pheasant, partridge, snipe and quail, he could escape his role as sparkling diva's dullish husband and play the *grand seigneur* to his heart's content. He was only just over forty when they bought the old castle and started to do it up. At that age he could spend all day on his blood sport and still enjoy a long evening of conversation and music around the piano with guests from all over Europe.

His young guest Ivan Turgenev shared his pleasure in hunting to the full. 'I will only ever feel truly happy,' he wrote to Louis on his return to Russia from Courtavenel (a little too effusively), 'when I can again roam the much-loved plains of Brie at your side, my gun in my hand . . .'

No wonder Turgenev felt inspired to write most of his *Hunter's Notes* here, early in his three-year sojourn at the castle, although all the stories in the collection (his first real book) were set in Russia. It's a book I've never taken to very strongly, although it remains one of his best-known and best-loved. Even Daniel, who has no particular interest in things Russian, vaguely recalled having read bits and pieces of it years before, possibly in an earlier incarnation. What had stayed in his mind, as in mine, were the pictures, not so much of hunting, which is often incidental to the stories he tells, as of the peasants (the serfs), all those Yakovs, Yermolais, Arinas, Nikolais, Petrushkas and Pavels, each one drawn with the same delicacy and depth as the serf-owners themselves. The whole book smells unforgettably of dogs, water, rotting thatch, wormwood, buckwheat, dead game, mud, drink and campfires. It rings to the sound of gunshot, shouting, flogging, birdcalls, peasants singing and frightened voices telling terrible stories. Already, at the outset of his writing career Turgenev had mastered the art, as Virginia Woolf noted in one of her delicately intelligent essays on the Russian writer, of combining the photograph and the poem. Others, as she says, are much better storytellers than Turgenev, but nobody surpasses him in this particular skill.

I didn't want to discuss hunting with a Buddhist, however, not feeling up to a monologue on karma or the doctrine of rebirth (Daniel wouldn't even swat flies), so I let the subject of hunting drop. As far as I'm concerned, slaughtering animals and birds for sport is simply an incomprehensible abomination, like child abuse or rape – in fact, very like child abuse and rape. The stalking of innocent prey in the company of a pack of excited males, the joy in shared animality, the targeting, the craving to pierce and possess, the ecstatic consummation, the subsequent relief and mournful languor . . . any description of a hunt as sport brings to mind sexual pursuit of the innocent.

Gunning down game has always been a gentleman's occupation, of course, and Turgenev was, after all, born a medieval squire with vast domains teeming with both wildlife and serfs to transport him from lair to lair, tend to his horse and fix broken axles on his cart. Even the troubadours hunted between bouts of mooning – right here, presumably, a short ride from Provins, where Countess Marie of Champagne held court. What else was there for them to do when they weren't wooing the lady of the castle? After all, they weren't about to plough or scythe or fight. Nevertheless, one might have expected that Turgenev of all people would have seen through and recoiled from this aspect of medieval life as he did from so many others – autocracy, slave-ownership and religious obscurantism to name just three.

The sort of hunting Ivan Sergeyevich so enjoyed was not the gruesome formal chase with hounds, conducted like a military campaign, even in Russia before the emancipation of the serfs, with thousands of hunters and armies of (sometimes liveried) peasants fanning out across the countryside, in some cases for weeks at a time. He hunted alone with a serf companion, as many Russian gentlemen did, almost on an equal footing with him, dressed almost indistinguishably from him, sharing meals with him and talking with him deep into the night less like a master than a friend. The pleasure of these escapes from his everyday life is no mystery. But why did they have to climax in an orgy of slaughter?

Anyone can understand the hunter's joy in feeling at one with nature, blissfully yielding to her in all her moods – tempestuous, smiling, sultry, mysterious, gay, buzzing with life. In fact, Turgenev makes you feel only half-alive sometimes, sitting (as you probably are while you turn the pages of *A Hunter's Notes*) in a chair in a room in a house in a suburb with nothing more natural for your eye to rest on than the family dog or a vase or flowers. But when a partridge flies up out of a birch-tree, or a flock of lapwings, crakes or orioles swoops by overhead, why does a gentle man like Turgenev, who went into raptures over Beethoven, Brahms and Romantic poetry, urgently want to kill them? Why does feeling at one with nature entail a desire to wipe it out?

———

In his slightly mawkish *Poems in Prose*, written over several years towards the end of his life, Turgenev reflects more than once on Nature as the mother we all share – birds, animals, human beings, even worms. There's nothing too remarkable about that. What is revealing, however, is his insistence that this common mother is also the pitiless exterminator of life, both human and animal – and that to her there is absolutely no distinction. A man, a worm – it's all the same to Nature. As part of nature, Turgenev may well have believed that he had no more moral obligation to cherish animal life than a wolf or bird does, although killing his own species for sport was obviously another matter.

Free to kill, he became an erotically aroused predator once he was out in the fields or the forest on the track of game. Although the erotic frenzy of much writing about killing wild animals is missing in his *Hunter's Notes*, there is definitely joy there. It's 'jolly fun' (*veselo*), he tells us, to watch dead ducks tumbling head over heels through the air and slapping down into the water. He kills '*dlya potekhi*' – 'just to have a bit of fun' – an expression which has the same sexual shading to it in Russian as it does in English. His heart is in an agony of longing and suspense (*tomitsa* – the word lovers use) as the woodcock, with a cry, swishes through the air towards the jutting barrel of his gun.

'He lived here for three years?' Daniel asked, a little incredulously, eyes on the road as the scratches and squiggles of Pécy turned into solid houses just ahead of us.

'On and off, yes. He went back and forth to Paris, of course, for the theatre and the opera and to see friends . . . and the revolution, he was in Paris for the events of 1848.' (Did young Frenchmen still know what had happened in 1848?)

'Still, three years is a long time. How old was he?'

'Thirtyish. He dropped in briefly for the first time while he was on a grand tour and then came back two years later and stayed. It was like a railway station, Courtavenel, everyone said so, with all the comings and goings. But no one stayed as long as Turgenev. He wrote several plays here – *A Month in the Country*, for example, have you seen it?'

He wasn't sure he'd ever heard of it. But before we could pursue it, like everyone else he had to get one thing straight: were Ivan Turgenev and Pauline Viardot lovers? What sort of a *ménage à trois* was this?

'Nobody knows,' I said.

'Somebody must know.'

'From their letters you really can't tell. If they ever did . . . you know, have relations' – a snappier phrase seemed inappropriate – 'then it probably *was* here at Courtavenel about two years after he arrived, most biographers seem to think. Some people believe one or two of her children might even have been his, but nobody knows. I actually find it quite hard to imagine, somehow. I suppose one sultry evening when Louis was away a kiss could have turned into . . .' (And here I thought of Litvinov and Irina in that luggage-room in the hotel in Baden-Baden, the loosened hair, the tinkling comb.) 'But – how can I put it? – I think it's the wrong question to ask.'

'What's wrong with it? It seems quite a reasonable question to me.' Eyes still on the road. Shaven head gleaming in the sun. I didn't know what to say.

'Okay, it's not the wrong question, but I do think it's beside the point. Or was for Turgenev. Or soon was – at least by the time he left Courtavenel. I'm not sure that for him love always needed to take that form. Or not first and foremost.'

Daniel didn't say anything, but I could tell he thought I was being wishy-washy and evasive. A passionate, strikingly good-looking single man in his early thirties who felt no need for sex with the woman he was crazy about?

'And the husband? Louis, was it?'

'Well, they seem to have stayed very good friends, judging by the letters they wrote to each other. Men's letters, you know . . . about *things,* mostly – hunting, music, money, politics. But there was a real warmth to them.'

Daniel, I suspect, had been hoping for something a little spicier, a little more inventive. Muddling about like most of his friends in the space between the lifelong twosome and libertinage, he was always canvassing options. I'd have liked to bring up triangles, but people usually bristle when you mention triangles – they automatically think of betrayal, rivalry, smirking winners and bitter losers – and I wasn't sure I was ready with the kind of nuanced vocabulary I'd need to discuss them at that moment. I'd wait until we were in a more relaxed setting.

I DOUBT THAT much active canvassing of options, apart from a spot of adultery, has ever taken place in Pécy, but I could be wrong. It was another very old town clustered, like Rozay-en-Brie, around an ancient church in the middle of the empty plain. It must have been like Siberia in winter. When we asked them about Courtavenel through the car-window, four very old men sitting in the sun beside the road burst into a hubbub of explanations, jabbing with their walking-sticks back the way we'd come. We'd just passed it, apparently, a minute or two before. I felt my whole body tighten with excitement. This was it! This was *the cradle of his fame* – as Turgenev himself called it. This is where he'd stopped scribbling derivative verse and become a real writer, where he'd felt a mad infatuation turn into love and first savoured 'civilisation' at any length . . . right here, somewhere near the white stone farmhouse slipping by across the field on our right. (Yet, maddeningly, not really 'here' at all, as I knew all too well.)

All of a sudden we both saw the sign to Courtavenel where the road to the farmhouse we'd just passed turned off ours. Swinging onto this straight, white country road, we made our way respectfully back across the fields towards the farmhouse and pulled up, a little gingerly, outside the yawning gateway in the high stone wall surrounding it.

There was utter silence when we stepped from the car, just the scrunching of our shoes on the gravel. And then a soft chirruping somewhere nearby. And I thought of something Turgenev once wrote about 'the fresh, bitter smell' and 'the serene melancholy' of the woods and fields around Courtavenel at the close of summer.

'I hope there aren't any savage dogs about,' Daniel said, looking around warily, but there were no signs of life at all. 'So is this what's left of the "castle", do you think? Is this Courtavenel?'

With its massive stone wall, high shingled roof and gateway leading through a tunnel to a courtyard inside, there was certainly something medieval about it to my eyes. The gateway only needed a portcullis to whisk you back eight hundred years. At the same time it managed to look brand spanking new. Which is what it was, more or less, as we were soon to find out.

While we were wondering what to do next, out of the shadows of the yawning portal emerged the farmer's wife – not, I hasten to add, a farmer's wife with so much as a whiff of the peasant about her. This was a Brie farmer's wife, who strode towards us beaming, every inch the lady of the manor. In a flash Daniel reinvented himself for the encounter.

In a flurry of subjunctives and courteous circumlocutions, he explained charmingly – his sunglasses held at the angle once reserved for those long, old-fashioned *fume-cigarettes* – that we were simply

THERE WAS INDEED NOTHING THERE. Instead of the fairytale castle I knew from Pauline's sketch, instead of elegant sixteenth-century turrets and conical spires, a grand entrance and drawbridge on the northern side (the 'noble' side, as Pauline called it) and respectable country estate façade to the south (the 'bourgeois', 'good-natured' side), there was nothing at all. In an even earlier sketch I'd seen of Courtavenel it had actually looked more like a busy village than a mere castle. All that remains is an empty mown square with bushes and trees around the edges, lining what was left of the old moat. We all stood on the old stone bridge over the moat (a dry ditch now), thinking our own thoughts and staring into the sunlit emptiness. Then, abruptly, I wanted to laugh.

It was here, not in Baden-Baden or the rue de Douai, but here, where there was nothing left at all, no plaques or busts or ruins or painstaking restorations, that I felt – *at last really felt* – and here I must tread very carefully to avoid the minefield of necromantic gobbledygook – that I was alive to Turgenev. *He* had not come alive – I had. And so I laughed.

'What's so funny?' Daniel asked with a grin, wanting to share the joke. I just shook my head. I couldn't explain. Not right then or right there.

What was I so suddenly alive to? It wasn't so much a matter of feeling prompted by this green emptiness to imagine even more vividly than before the life the young Turgenev had once lived there – re-arranging Louis' library while a servant waxed the furniture; exercising the dogs; rowing yet another famous guest around the moat; dancing at one of the parties in the banquet hall (Ivan Sergeyevich loved to dance); telling stories to the family in the evening as they sewed and knitted, with Gounod working on a new score over by the fire; setting off with Louis to hunt quail on a fine autumn morning; waking up from one of his blood-freezing nightmares about monsters rising from the deep to devour him; brushing against spirits on the staircase in the night; spiralling up (or down) into a love that had no proper name – no, it wasn't a matter of feeling prompted to imagine any of this more vividly, although it made me dizzy just to look at that green square. I'd pictured all those things to myself before. I'd needed to, obviously, in order to listen to his voice with understanding as I read him.

No, what I felt suddenly alive to was something else. Now in Courtavenel I could sense why, when he arrived here for the first time as a young man in 1845, he must have felt both that *he had come home at last, yet at the same time belonged not here, but somewhere else.* And this contradiction coloured every syllable he later wrote.

Civilisation – here it was, at last! He'd been to Berlin and Paris by this time, of course, as well as Rome and dozens of other great cities from Bordeaux to Naples, but Courtavenel – way out on this plain of beetroot and barley! – must have struck him as the distillation of every notion of civilisation to enter a European head since the Greeks. Not in those words, naturally, but I could imagine him rattling along that last straight stretch of road in his tilbury, chestnut hair flying, eyes fixed on the *château* directly ahead, every inch the young troubadour approaching his unapproachable lady, thinking to himself: here it is at last – this is it, *in a nutshell*. If there was no lion and unicorn carved above the portal, then there should have been.

You may have to be antipodean, or at least Russian – from beyond the boundary stones of the civilised world, at any rate – to feel this contradiction in your very bones. I can recall my own emotions in 1965 when for the first time France appeared through the clouds far below me. I hadn't yet seen Paris, Berlin or Rome. I had seen New York and Los Angeles, but they had turned out to be merely larger, wealthier versions of what I already knew, they weren't *civilisation*, as the patchwork of fields, roads and townships with spires below me were. *Civilisation* was something else, and had been since the days of Periclean Athens. I'd know it when I saw it and I saw it when the plane crossed the coast of France. When the young Turgenev first set eyes on Courtavenel, he, too, must have been convinced that he was looking at its very embodiment.

IN GREEK TERMS, both Ivan Sergeyevich and I were Persians – or, in my case, something even more outlandish: a Phrygian, let's say, or even a Scythian from beyond the Black Sea. After all, I came quite literally from a land of monsters, a continent thought until quite recently to be teeming with half-hounds, one-eyed freaks and men who used their feet as umbrellas. There are pictures of them on old maps. Turgenev came from a land much closer to the boundary stones than mine, but still from beyond that belt of half-civilised Slav tribes on the edges of Europe – Poles, Ukrainians, Byelorussians and so on. Or is Russia beyond a belt of Lapps and Turks? The geography can be confusing. As the Marquis de Custine reported after a journey to Russia in 1839 (the year after Turgenev had first left for abroad), 'Russia in the present age is only 400 years removed from the invasion of barbarian tribes' – he meant the Tartars – 'while it is 1,400 years since Western Europeans went through the same crisis. Civilisation which has lasted over a thousand years longer [in one place than another] will naturally put an immeasurable distance between the manners of nations.' Even before the Tartar invasion, the Marquis reminded his readers, 'Russia had received its rulers from Scandinavia and they in turn had adopted their tastes, arts and luxuries from the emperors and patriarchs of Constantinople.' In the end, civilisation always turns out to be Greek.

According to the Greeks in the fifth century BC, civilisation was first and foremost about speaking Greek, not babbling away in some outlandish foreign tongue, such as Persian. (Turgenev and I both made it our business to learn 'Greek' well when we were small children. You never quite pass, of course – a 'Persian' vowel here, a 'Scythian' construction there. You can never erase all trace of your barbarian origins.) Civilisation was also about the close-knit *rootedness* of your culture, so it was about stone cities, paved streets and palaces, not muddy settlements of wooden huts. It was about cultivated fields, not untamed nature.

Barbarians, on the other hand, tended to wander mindlessly about their wild landscapes, indulging in a spot of rapine from time to time, with their families packed into carts, followed by herds of sheep and cattle. In Australia our nomadic past is so recent you'll occasionally even see one of these carts going for a song in a country junk-shop.

In Russia, even in Turgenev's day, nomadism was always lurking just beneath the surface, the towns being little more than flimsy stage-sets. Even the palaces – copied, by the way, from Italians inspired in turn by their classical heritage – were basically just stucco on wood. No wonder the fire that broke out the night Napoleon marched into Moscow reduced three-quarters of the city to ashes in under a week. In 1829, when Turgenev was just eleven, the thinker Chaadayev famously wrote in the first of his *Philosophical Letters*: 'We [Russians] all have the appearance of people on the move . . . We have no sense of hearth and home, there's nothing to attach us to anything . . . In our houses we live as if we were billeting, in our own families we seem like people from somewhere else, while in our towns we are even more like nomads than the nomads themselves, grazing their flocks on our steppes, because they are more closely bound to their wilderness than we are to our cities.'

A civilised society valued learning, too, as well as honed intellects, contemplation and the arts, rather than the unrefined emotions and mere brute strength a pillaging barbarian needed to survive. It encouraged set virtues in its citizens – temperance, a sense of justice, wisdom – although the Greeks did make allowances for unruly behaviour in young men. To my youthful perception, the country I came to France from, constantly characterised as 'young', had rather too much respect for extravagant displays of physical prowess, its heroes usually being footballers, cricketers and men of action, while our poets, intellectuals and artists, anyone who might want to contemplate the drift of history and ideas, were little more than a frivolous sideshow to the main events. To this day, needless to say, the Australians whose names are most likely to appear in the European press are our tennis players, swimmers and popular entertainers, not our scientists or thinkers. Our most famous cultural export to Great Britain is almost certainly Barry Humphries, the civilised barbarian who became a superstar by aping barbarians aping the civilised.

In terms of honed intellects and the arts, Russians have been much more successful than we have at beating the civilised at their own game – or appearing to do so, despite the firestorms of inhumanity that swept the country in both tsarist and modern times. When most people think 'Russia' these days, I imagine they think Tolstoy,

Dostoyevsky, *Swan Lake* at the Bolshoi, Prokofiev, Rostropovich, Eisenstein, Tarkovsky, the Trans-Siberian railway, the first sputniks . . . God knows what they think, actually, but I doubt they begin by thinking 'White Sea Canal', 'Magadan', 'death-camps', 'slave labour'. And if the thought of 'mass murder on a scale never before seen on the face of the planet' pops into their heads, they can always think 'Solzhenitsyn', 'Akhmatova' or perhaps 'Pasternak', vaguely recalling unpleasantnesses over his *Doctor Zhivago*.

In a word, from the Greek point of view civilised men and women are rational adults inhabiting a rationally organised landscape, while barbarians are irrational children, always on the verge of running wild. Ultimately, it's an argument about time. To be civilised means not to be confined to your own time, but to be aware of time's sweep and convolutions. Yet, as Chaadayev wrote about Russians in his 1829 letter: 'Standing as it were outside time, we have not been touched by humankind's cultivation of knowledge . . . everything flows on, everything passes away, leaving no trace either in us or our surroundings.' In *The Coast of Utopia* Stoppard has the revolutionary, Herzen (one of Turgenev's friends, until they quarrelled), put it slightly differently: 'Civilisation passed us by,' he says to Bakunin, 'we belonged to geography, not history . . .' When I went to school in Sydney, my country was also just 'geography', a space. There was no such subject as Australian history. History meant the French Revolution, the American Civil War, the British kings and queens, even recent upheavals in China, but it was not a concept that we applied to Australia. 'So we escaped,' as Stoppard's Herzen says about his generation of Russians.

You had to.

Growing up as Turgenev and I both did, beyond the boundary stones of civilisation, beyond time, if you could read and think, you realised in your teenage years that, however well-fed you were, however available all the conveniences of modern life, however pleasant the life you were leading beyond the purview of the Greeks of the day, you were nevertheless at best a Persian – not necessarily barbaric, mind, not personally an out-and-out savage, but, compared to the Greeks, uncivilised.

Nowadays the whole notion of boundary stones has begun to fade, along with distance in general. Barbarians are now simply the folk from the wrong side of the tracks, whatever country they live in, not from the wrong side of the Black Sea or the Danube. Even now, though, in the twenty-first century, I am conscious of how little 'Greek' attitudes have changed since the days when Agatha Christie could write without blushing (it was 1922): 'My own sketchy ideas of Australia comprised kangaroos in large quantities, and a great deal of waste desert.' In the same year D.H. Lawrence wrote to his sister-in-law back in England: 'You never knew anything so nothing, nichts, nullus, niente, as the life here . . . your inner self dies out, and you clatter round like so many mechanical animals.' Not a society, but a collection of animals in a wasteland. Even today Greek taxi-drivers who can barely read and write will assure me that Australia 'has no culture' – it's sunny and good for getting rich in, but hardly 'civilised'. Some Russians, too, arriving in Australia to take advantage of the high standard of living, can be just as withering: '*Odno beskulturye*' ('A complete lack of culture'), they'll say, drifting off on some neo-classical Soviet dream they were brought up on of the civilised society. It's a country run by philistines, naturally, as most countries seem to be, but it's not in the outer darkness, unlit by the sun shining down on 'Greece'. Some suburbs are, but not the country. We've been globalised.

———

Forty or fifty years ago, however, by the time you reached adulthood, you had to run with the herd or else, like Herzen, escape. What you were escaping from was often as much the rude opinions of other people as any real lack of civilisation: if you had any pretensions to civilised thought, you were usually seen by those around you as a misfit – an ugly duckling, a fop, an effete poseur, someone with ideas above his station. Turgenev, too, at the age of twenty was widely thought of as a 'dandy' – an amusing raconteur, quite brilliant in his way, but a butterfly, a mere aesthete, lacking in substance. He for his part found Russian society, with its feudal system of masters and slaves, inhumane and disgusting. 'Nearly everything I saw,' he wrote later, 'roused feelings in me of shame and indignation – of revulsion, in fact.' So he fled, initially, at least, to Berlin to study, Germany in the 1830s being where Europe's most highly honed intellects did their thinking.

Apart from anything else, we were impatient at twenty to get to the source of all those things that made the civilised what they were and us something else. We were tired of living in a hand-me-down world. As Chaadayev noted in desperation in 1829: 'we've never bothered to think up anything for ourselves, yet, from what others have thought up, we've only taken over the deceptive, external things and useless luxuries.' No wonder Turgenev, homing in on the artistic aspect of civilisation, believed that the sign of a civilised country was the autonomy of its art. Absolute autonomy is surely a mirage, even the folk-dancing on some remote Pacific atoll will turn out to have been influenced by the folk-dancing on another atoll, which, in turn . . . and so on. But a civilised country does not simply fill its bookshops, art galleries, theatres, cinemas and airwaves with some other society's cultural product. You know what Turgenev meant.

Where we fled to in those days depended on where we came from and what we'd been reading. When another misfit, Katherine Mansfield, was a young girl in Wellington at the turn of the century, for instance, dreaming feverishly of escaping the provincial tedium of the New Zealand capital (and her unhappy home life), she fixed romantically on Russia as the place where her turbulent inner life would find the appreciation it deserved and be allowed to express itself in suitably exotic surroundings. (Restless young barbarians generally talk a lot about 'being appreciated'.) It was in fact the novels of Turgenev and Tolstoy, as well as the music of Tchaikovsky, Anton Rubinstein and a host of other 'Slavonic' composers, which gave Russia its aura of 'civilisation' for the adolescent Katherine Mansfield. (Her passion for Chekhov came later.) In other words, it was Europe, filtered through the culture of Russia's refined elite, which promised escape.

What drew Katherine most powerfully to the Russians was the sense that in them she had found larger, more articulate, more self-possessed versions of who she thought she really was – an irresistible illusion when you're young. When Diaghilev brought a dazzling exhibition of Russian modernist art to Paris in 1906, she must have felt rapturously vindicated. A year later he pulled Chaliapin, Rachmaninov and Rimsky-Korsakov out of a hat, and soon after that Anna Pavlova and Nijinski. Savagery plus sensibility – Europe was agog. If Potugin (Litvinov's grumpy friend in *Smoke*) had been in Paris at that time, he'd almost certainly have dismissed the Diaghilev circus with an arthritic wave of his walking-stick as no more 'Russian' than harpsichords or Haydn – or than Turgenev, for that matter. Ivan Sergeyevich himself, though, if he'd lived to see it, might have thought it was all 'autonomously' Russian to just the right degree. As Stoppard has him put it in *The Coast of Utopia*: 'The only thing that'll save Russia is western culture transmitted by . . . people like us.'

It's hard at this distance for me to recall in any detail what I thought of the country I was leaving in 1965 or what I thought I was 'coming home to' as the plane came in to land at Orly. I did not feel anything akin to Turgenev's revulsion for my native land – why would I have? It was hardly a feudal autocracy with 'not a single useful idea' to its credit, as Chaadayev claimed Russia was at the time. Nor did I feel a complete alien in my own land, as Katherine Mansfield seems to have done in New Zealand, a stray piece of jetsam from a passing British liner. Not at all. By the same token, when I came across that passage in *Kangaroo* recently where Lawrence describes some boys on a beach near Sydney in the early 1920s 'lunging about' (it's the 'about' that's so telling) like 'real young animals, mindless as opossums', I was struck by how deftly he had captured in just a few words the way in which Europeans once thought of my country: a space devoid of intellect, empty of meaning. It was much the way I once thought of it myself. 'Vacant' (Lawrence's word) except for a few disorderly children making shrill noises in the lap of nature. His central character, the Englishman Somers, says he'd feel more at home with any lout on the streets of Naples than with these barbarians. (Many of us, too, have made fools of ourselves with Neopolitan louts we wouldn't have given a second thought to if they'd been home-grown Australians.)

In short: this was Phrygia in every respect. In one letter home

Lawrence wrote that being in Australia was 'rather like falling out of a picture and finding oneself on the floor, with all the gods and men left behind in the picture'. Not by nature a real young animal, mindless as an opossum, I was desperate by the age of twenty-one to get up off the floor and back into that picture – back into time and history.

———

None of this would have been easy to explain to Daniel, for all his trips to the civilisations of the East, when he asked me 'what was so funny'. Perhaps I would try on the way back to Paris in the long twilight. It was the laughter of connivance, I would have to say to him – with Turgenev, not with you. It was a tacit accord between two young barbarians. I laughed because that moment of recognition which I think Ivan Sergeyevich must have experienced on the approach to Courtavenel was one I knew all about. In both our cases, love had been, if not blind, then at least short-sighted. And, like him, I eventually had to leave because I actually belonged somewhere else.

'Barbarian? But you're not a barbarian,' Daniel would say (I hoped). 'You speak French and Russian, you write books, you've read Diderot and Dante and Dostoyevsky, you live in a democratic country with opera houses and . . .' *(Slight pause.)*

'Airports? Law courts? Cappuccinos?'

'Why are you taking that tone?'

'Because all you're saying is that I can pass for one of you.' And now I imagined him thinking to himself: *Not quite, my friend.* And that would peeve me (because it was true, although that shouldn't matter, but it did), and I would lapse into a sulky silence. Was I starting to play Dostoyevsky to my own Turgenev?

Why even bother trying to explain to a Parisian why somebody like me, forty years earlier, would have felt he was a barbarian; why I'd felt I was coming home when I stepped onto the tarmac at Orly airport; why I'd *recognised* the Paris I'd never seen in a way he obviously could never recognise Sydney or Hobart; why I was so elated by the rootedness in Paris of all the transplanted things I'd taught myself to love; why I also knew I did not belong there and would one day have to leave; and why I now thought the boundary stones of civilisation were just a mirage. He was a Greek, I was a Phrygian, and that was that. This particular game was played by his rules.

Dostoyevsky proposed playing a different game altogether in order to sort out the sheep from the goats: instead of Civilisation vs. Barbarism, he suggested Orthodoxy vs. Paganism (socialism, Catholicism – anything that wasn't Russian Orthodox, it was all essentially the same). I could hardly play that game and win, though, having had no training in it. At the Muslim vs. Christian game, another possibility, I was hardly even a spectator. That interesting Greek librarian, Eratosthenes of Alexandria, who calculated the earth's circumference 200 years before our era, mischievously suggested that it would be better to divide people into the Good and the Bad, surely, rather than Greeks and Barbarians, 'since many Greeks are bad, and many barbarians civilised, particularly the Indians and the Arians, as well as the Romans and Carthaginians, who enjoy such admirable forms of government'. But do you in fact have to play team sports at all?

———

'Would you like to take a walk over there where the castle stood?' The farmer's wife was smiling at me, wondering where I'd drifted off to. We were still standing on the stone bridge across the moat. I'd forgotten where I was. Daniel had turned his head to look at me, too, with a quizzical expression on his face.

'No, no, thank you,' I said, immediately sure I did not want to step onto the green square. What would be the point? Even if I did trip over a piece of the grey marble fireplace they'd all gathered around of an evening, or stumble into a tangle of gooseberry bushes from the old front garden, what would be the point? I wasn't looking for holy relics.

'WE MUSTN'T KEEP YOU ANY LONGER,' I said, after taking a few photographs of the green square, just to show I was seriously impressed by it. 'You've been extraordinarily kind. Don't you get tired of people wanting to see where the castle was?'

'To tell you the truth, hardly anyone gets this far,' she said, turning to go back into the tunnel. 'A few Russians, that's all. This gateway was here in the Viardots' day, by the way,' she said, disappearing ahead of us into the shadows, 'like the stone bridge, although we've rebuilt around it, as you can see.'

Really? When the carriage came for Turgenev on the last morning, in the summer of 1850, to bear him away sobbing to Rozay-en-Brie, and then to Paris and finally Russia, was this the way he came? Through this tunnelled gateway? Were these walls of tightly packed small stones, echoing to our footsteps, the selfsame walls he saw that morning in his misery? He'd have been clutching his dappled English setter, Diana, as he clattered by. I reached out and touched them. They were cold and dry.

What a ghastly morning it must have been. After three years in France, he was returning to Russia – forever, as far as he knew at the time.

'My whole being,' he wrote to Pauline when he got to Paris that evening, 'can be summed up in a single word: adieu – adieu.' (Is the repetition therefore heart-breaking or an amusing mistake?) He was leaving quite suddenly, too, in great emotional turmoil, having written to Pauline in London only three days earlier to tell her that he was going home. For much of the time during those three years he'd stayed on at Courtavenel even when Pauline was away on tour, as she was on the morning he left. He had come and gone to Paris, travelled around the region, and sometimes even further afield, but for the best part of three years Courtavenel had been his home. It was here that he wrote his first mature works (his plays and A Hunter's Notes), here that his love for Pauline Viardot matured, here, in a sense, that he grew up. And it was here, by that summer of 1850, that it had become apparent, I take it – to our troubadour, his mistress and definitely her husband – that, whatever intimacies had occurred the previous summer, what he had by now was all he was going to get. Not quite enough for a man in his early thirties, yet there was no prospect of much more. If Louis, who was now middle-aged, had shown some sign of conveniently wasting away, perhaps Ivan would have persevered, but there was nothing decrepit about Louis. In other words, while love was possible, this particular expression of it was going nowhere.

Pauline was probably not heart-broken to see him go. Exactly what her husband really felt we shall never know, but it was not deep regret. Although she was physically attracted to her barbarian admirer (she said so), it's worth considering that Pauline almost certainly found some things about him off-putting, too off-putting to allow her to draw closer. She kept referring to him as a '*sauvage*', for instance, which was not a good sign. Indeed, there may have been things about him she actively disliked, insurmountable things, which, as we all know, can range from the way somebody slurps his soup to deeply rooted personality flaws. And Pauline Viardot, after all, was in a position to choose – that's partly why she was so attractive to him in the first place.

Perhaps, too, she'd tired of being loved unquestioningly. Being loved without reservation or respite can become humdrum, like blinking or breathing. Besides, by this time she was infatuated with the fetching young Charles Gounod, a sort of French version of Turgenev (they were the same age and both slightly cloying) who had installed himself with his mother, alongside Ivan Sergeyevich, at Courtavenel to compose his opera *Sapho* (with a part for Pauline). She was so obviously infatuated, indeed, that some scorpion-tongues spoke of the triangle having become a square. The dignified thing for Turgenev to do was to leave. (*Sapho*, it's worth recording, turned out to be a flop.)

His letter to '*chère, bonne Madame Viardot*' written from Paris late at night on 24 June is anguished. 'I look around me,' he wrote to her, in terms we might find it hard not to think of as self-pitying (but should not, I think):

> *and gather my memories to me, even the most insignificant of them, as emigrants to America are said to gather about them even the humblest of their household belongings, and I will take them all away with me like a treasure. If you were willing to promise me . . . that you would remember me, I think I might be able to bear the absence more easily – with a less heavy heart. When you get back to Courtavenel, promise me*

that you will greet its cherished walls in my name. When,
sitting together on the steps in front of the house on a fine
autumn evening, watching the tops of the poplars stirring . . .
think, I beg of you, of your absent friend, who would have
been so happy to be among you. As for me, I have no need to
promise you that I'll be thinking of you often, it's all I will be
doing. I can see myself from here, sitting alone under the old
lime-trees in my garden, my face turned towards France,
murmuring softly: where are they? what are they doing now?
Ah! I'm leaving my heart here, I know that only too well . . .

He continued the next morning, after a sleepless night:

My head is on fire. I am overcome with fatigue and distress. I
have been weeping while packing my bags – I can't collect my
thoughts – I really don't know what I'm writing. I've sent you
my address. I'll write to you from Berlin. Adieu – adieu. I kiss
all of you – you, Viardot – bless all of you – my dear, good
friends, my only family, you whom I love more than anything
else in the world . . . It's time for me to close now – it's time –
it's time. Very well, then, courage! Let's not lose hope. Let me
take you in my arms again for the last time, let me press you to
my heart, my good, my dear friends – the heart that loves you
so much. I leave you in God's care. May you be happy. I love
you and will love you until the end of my life. . . .

Your I. Turgenev

And he did, in the most remarkable fashion.

Ivan and Pauline were not to meet again for six years, apart from a brief, and illegal, rendezvous in Moscow in 1853 while Pauline was on tour and he was living in enforced exile on his estate at Spasskoye. (He had infuriated the tsar with an article he'd published in which he'd called Gogol 'great'. His punishment was exile.)

His letters to her during the first years of separation were dotted with the usual endearments – he confessed to wishing he could spend his whole life as a carpet beneath her feet, assured her that he belonged to her and her alone entirely (which wasn't quite true), kissed her feet 'for hours on end' – and thanked her for sending him her fingernail parings (in return for which he sent her his illegitimate daughter to look after).

But when they did meet again at the castle in 1856 (the tsar had meanwhile died and Turgenev had been granted permission to travel abroad again), although he said he felt as happy as a trout in a clear stream bathed in sunlight, something had begun to die. Amateur theatricals in the little theatre set up in the attic (admission: one potato), hunting with the ever-affable Louis, Beethoven sonatas on the piano, dinner parties with guests from all over Europe, sketching expeditions into the surrounding countryside – it was all very merry, but it was simply the merriment of the entr'acte. In reality the curtain had come down on the first act six years before – the shooting, plays and sonatas were just an entertainment before the second. Pauline's mind was by this time elsewhere.

———

When he came back to Courtavenel in 1859, for another few weeks, it was clear that something had died. 'I look at my youth,' Turgenev wrote to a friend on this final visit, 'as at someone else's youth and happiness. I am here and all that is over there, and between the *here* and the *there* is an abyss which nothing will ever fill in all eternity.'

It was time, in other words, if his passionate adoration for Pauline Viardot were not to become a mere memory, for it to ripen into something else entirely. It would be a matter, as it generally is, even in marriages, of having the wit to switch genres, like recasting an opera as a ballet or a poem as a painting. And amazingly this happened, although not all at once.

ONE THING I COULDN'T HELP reflecting on as we set off back to
Paris was the fact that nowhere in all the novels or short stories he
went on to write after leaving Courtavenel is there a portrait of Pauline
Viardot. Not even a thumbnail sketch. Why? Is it because the living
Pauline was too deeply woven into his very being to be plucked out
and turned into a character in a story, as a woman glimpsed in a rail-
way-carriage or a passing infatuation might be? Is it because, in some
way not at all as trivial as I'm making it sound, his love for Viardot was
literally beyond words – beyond retelling, beyond encapsulating in a
storyline with beginning, middle and end? Perhaps, I thought to
myself as we drove westwards along the empty road through patches
of forest, Pauline's absence from his stories was not as strange as it at
first seemed. All sorts of characters from my own past have made an
appearance in my writing, from my wife (once the marriage was over)
to people I'd met briefly on park benches, from chance dinner companions to passing objects of desire, but the most beloved of those I've

loved, my second self, is nowhere to be seen in my fiction. Or ever likely to be.

———

In Rozay-en-Brie, where Turgenev and his dog would have waited forlornly that June morning for the diligence to Paris, Daniel parked the car near the forbidding, ancient church on the main street and we went into the brasserie nearby for coffee and a cheesy *croque*. We'd hardly spoken since Courtavenel and needed to reconnect, eye to eye, which is difficult in the front seat of a car. Where my feeling of slight ennui came from, I'm not sure – the flatness of the landscape, probably, as much as any melancholy thoughts about Turgenev. It was that funny late-afternoon feeling I have sometimes of being simultaneously empty and full to overflowing, both needy and replete.

'Did you enjoy that?' I asked him, once we'd settled in the almost empty brasserie and had time to take in the card-players in one corner and the blind man from the wedding holding court in another. 'Are you pleased you came?' I couldn't help wondering what the afternoon had given him.

'Very pleased,' he said, nodding to show he meant it. I hoped he might say more – ask some questions, comment on the farmer's wife, the moat, the landscape, anything – but he didn't, not just then. Was he being monkish and Himalayan? Perhaps, as Virginia Woolf once wrote of Turgenev's prose, the meaning of what he'd said went on after the sound had stopped.

Even on the way back to Paris we didn't say much. The light faded, the traffic thickened, the city sprang up like a forest and swallowed us up. It was only much later, after dinner when we were walking back to the Marais, that all the odd fragments making up our day seemed to shake down into patterns we needed words for. By the time we got to the square in front of Notre Dame, alive towards midnight with singers, street musicians, strollers and canoodling couples, we were skipping from *A Month in the Country* to Gounod's music, Henry James, the Chinese idea of barbarism (a little different from the Greek), the South Pacific ('Any desire to visit Australia one day?' A pause. 'Not really . . . Should I have?'), Hinduism . . . and then we sat in contented silence for a while and watched the young crowd milling about in front of the cathedral, its façade ablaze with white light. It was awe-inspiring. What Chinese visitors make of it I can't say, but Kenneth Clark, on the first page of his *Civilisation*, calls it 'the most rigorously intellectual façade in the whole of Gothic art'. For generations of pilgrims from the New World and beyond, as Clark says, it stands 'at the very centre of civilisation'. Light, confidence, beauty, reason, equilibrium, myth, power, history, stone.

'*Regarde nous, les nouveaux barbares,*' Daniel said with one of his disarming smiles, gesturing at the noisy throng of happy heathens dancing, drinking and strumming their guitars in the light from the façade. '*On est là, en train de s'amuser.*'

We didn't get onto the question of love until Notre Dame was well behind us and we were mingling with the smart-looking crowds spilling out of the bars of the Marais. In a cramped, smoky cellar we were passing, a woman was singing in Portuguese to lute and guitar. If that won't thicken the blood, nothing will. Besides, as I'd noticed once or twice before, Daniel can be much less monklike after midnight.

BOUGIVAL

WHEN YOU FIRST HEAR the name 'Bougival', what comes to mind? The Seine, perhaps. The outskirts of Paris. Maybe nothing at all. Nowadays 'Bougival' doesn't ring many bells. Even Daniel, who claims to know Paris 'like my own pocket', said: *'Bougival? C'est où exactement?'*

A hundred years ago or more, someone like Daniel would have known precisely where Bougival was. Well into the 1880s that whole stretch of the Seine from Argenteuil to Bougival was a playground for young Parisians, especially on Sundays. They went boating there, they bathed, they sketched and painted, they lunched in the riverside cafés, they watched regattas and strolled along the riverbank, they picnicked on the grass and dozed in hammocks beneath the trees, they even danced outdoors by the water's edge. Then, when evening fell, they caught the train back to town. And they did all this practically within sight of Turgenev's windows on the forested hillside above the river.

It's easy to picture Bougival in vivid colour because it was, as the Goncourts put it, 'the landscape studio of the modern French school', so we've all grown up with Bougival unawares. Kenneth Clark is even more precise: 'the riverside café of La Grenouillère', he says, referring to paintings by Renoir and Monet which most of us have seen at some time or other, 'is the birthplace of Impressionism'.

La Grenouillère is just a stone's throw upstream from Bougival. The flickering water (green, blue, yellow), the rippling reflections of trees and sun, the women's luminous dresses, the intense softness of the world, the glow of pleasure in which the amblers, diners, picnickers and boaters are bathed (a pleasure not captured in paint, some would say, since Pompeii) – we know all this not only from the Renoirs and Monets we have seen over the years, but from Pissarro, Sisley and a host of minor painters who haunted these gentle riverbanks while Turgenev was living at Bougival, transforming our ideas of what a good painting is – and what beauty is, for that matter.

The first time I ever went to Bougival, I remember, I had only the vaguest inkling of its Impressionist connections, so no specific paintings came to mind when I got there. It wasn't a matter of picturing in my mind's eye Renoir's *Boaters on the Seine at Bougival*, say (a burst of blue and green brushstrokes, tinged with yellow – 'a festival of the senses', in one critic's words), or one of those luncheon parties he liked to paint, the men in sweat-shirts and yellow hats, the women in bright dresses, at ease, flirtatious, gathered around a table under a striped awning, all radiantly hedonistic, you can smell the bouillabaisse, taste the cider. No, my memory for particular paintings is strictly an amateur's. I do remember thinking, though, as I wandered along the main road looking for Turgenev's house, that the scene on my left, along the river, 'looked like an Impressionist painting'. The caressing colours were the same. Some of the gentleness was still there. It was the kind of unspectacular beauty you have to be taught to see.

It wasn't what I'd expected to find: 'Bougival' had always rung a rather melancholy bell for me. It was where Turgenev spent a large part of his last years, after all, in the chalet he'd built for himself behind the mansion the Viardots had bought. This was where he grew distressingly ill and died.

It was mostly the summer months they all spent at Bougival – by about November they generally headed back to the rue de Douai in town. (In those days Paris was only three-quarters of an hour away by train and tram from a stop right in front of the villa.) Even so, the stories he wrote there had little of the Impressionists' Bougival about them, none of the radiance of those summery Sundays on the river. There's a gleam to some of them, certainly, a burnished quality, but it's the gleam of a knifeblade or necklace caught in lamplight.

I never found the house on that first occasion, and that's probably just as well. In those days, in the mid-seventies, it was still a ruin. As a matter of fact, looking back, I wonder what I thought I was doing, wandering around Bougival in search of it. Did I think I was there on some kind of pilgrimage? Was I foolishly hoping to touch a gate or doorknob *he* had touched and be healed? (By which I mean 'transcend something'. To have a point, a pilgrimage must surely give you at least the illusion of transcending something: your everyday self, for instance, or some of those things that hem you in, such as time or the awareness of mortality – whatever you need most urgently to transcend when you arrive at the shrine.) If so, it would, I'm sure have been a pointless exercise.

There is not much about Bougival today, however, to remind you of the Impressionists. It looks now much like any other riverside township on the outskirts of the metropolis: a string of shops, hotels, apartment buildings and service stations on one side of the road and boats moored on the narrow river on the other. It's prettier, I suppose, than a lot of the Parisian *banlieue*, but the vision of lush green hillsides in Sisley's *Les Coteaux de Bougival*, for instance, with just a few houses lost amongst the trees, would be difficult to recapture. That picture was actually painted the year Turgenev moved there in 1875.

I dare say if you narrowed your eyes, blocked your ears and brought to mind *La Seine à Bougival*, Monet's dreamy, mauvish view across a bridge to a scattering of pale, red-roofed houses nestling beside the water beneath forested hills, you might just contrive to recognise the township. Perhaps, for instance, in the early evening, from further up the hill where the restored chalet stands, once the traffic streaming along the N13 (at this point called the rue Tourguéneff) had thinned, you might just be able to imagine yourself back in Guy de Maupassant's Bougival. There's a scene in *Yvette*, written just after Turgenev died, which sounds almost as if he had his friend Turgenev's house in mind when he wrote it:

> They had set the table on the veranda which overlooked the river. The Printemps villa . . . was halfway up the hillside, just on the curve of the Seine, which turned in front of the garden wall and flowed towards Marly.
>
> Across from the residence, the island of Croissy formed a horizon of tall trees, a mass of greenery, and a long stretch of the wide river was visible, as far as the floating café of La Grenouillère, hidden beneath the foliage.
>
> Evening was falling, one of those calm evenings by the water, colourful and soft, one of those peaceful evenings which make you feel happy. Not a breath of air stirred the branches, not a shiver of wind ruffled the smooth, clear

surface of the Seine. It was not too hot, however, it was warm – it felt good to be alive. The invigorating coolness of the banks of the Seine rose towards a serene sky.

The sun was disappearing behind the trees on its way to other lands, and one had the impression of breathing in the peace and quiet of the already sleeping earth, of inhaling, in the peacefulness of the surroundings, the imperturbable life of the infinite.

As they left the drawing-room to sit at the table everyone was feeling elated. Their hearts were filled with gentleness and good spirits, they felt that it was going to be so delightful to dine there, out in the country, with this great river and this fading light as a setting, breathing this clear, sweet-smelling air . . .

THE AIR WAS NOT NOTICEABLY CLEAR and sweet-smelling the morning we parked the car just off the N13 at Bougival, although it was sunny in a hazy, late summer sort of way. It was a week or so after our trip to Courtavenel. Daniel had surprised me by announcing on the telephone a day or two before that he was 'reading your Turgenev'.

'Really?' I said. On the Courtavenel trip he hadn't given me the impression of being more than politely interested in my pursuit of Turgenev. 'What are you reading?'

'*Virgin Soil* – that's all they had, apart from *A Hunter's Notes.*' These days Daniel would never choose to read a book about killing birds and animals, however pivotal it had been in emancipating the serfs.

'Are you enjoying it?'

'Not particularly, no,' he said. 'Not yet, anyway.'

That was hardly surprising – I hadn't much cared for it myself the first time I'd read it (when I was about Daniel's age). It was a gloomy novel, this last and longest novel of his, a bit too mired in historical events nobody knew anything about any more (the failed attempt by young radicals in the late 1860s to rouse the peasants to revolt), without all the melodrama, prophecy and hysterical metaphysics which made novels like Dostoyevsky's *The Devils* so timelessly appealing – at least to academics and adolescents.

'Ah,' I said, thinking that a lift to Bougival was probably now out of the question. 'Perhaps you should've started with something more . . .' – always hard not to sound patronising in these situations, but why should a young Parisian computer technician be interested in the failure of a few quixotic Russian intellectuals to get a peasant revolt brewing in 1868? – 'well, something like *Torrents of Spring*, say, or *First Love*.' He might find the strong sexual undercurrent in these stories engaging, I thought, even if he found them rather dated.

'Oh, I'll keep reading it,' he said. 'I'm not bored. I just don't think it's very well-written.'

He wasn't alone in that. Virginia Woolf, an ardent admirer, once wrote that Turgenev 'often tells a story very badly', and she was right. What she meant by that, though, was quite illuminating: a good storyteller, according to Woolf, 'sees his book as a succession of events'. Turgenev, she said, saw each book 'as a succession of emotions radiating from some character at the centre . . . The connexion is not of events but of emotions, and if at the end of the book we feel a sense of completeness, it must be that in spite of his defects as a storyteller Turgenev's ear for emotion was so fine that . . . all is held together by the truth of his insight.' A fine ear for emotion was not something that much excited Russian critics in the 1870s and nothing Turgenev wrote, not even *Fathers and Sons*, was abused quite as viciously as *Virgin Soil*. Foaming at the lips, one reviewer wrote that the author was like an impotent old man who just couldn't leave young girls alone. 'Impotent' I understand, but what exactly did he mean by 'young girls'?

'So what are your plans for the weekend?' Daniel asked. That's when I mentioned wanting to visit Bougival, where *Virgin Soil* was in fact written, and he asked where it was.

'Not far,' I said. 'On the Seine. Quite close to Versailles, as a matter of fact. Ten kilometres away at the most.'

'Well, let's go on Sunday, then,' he said. Perfect. Sunday happened to be the only day you could visit the museum set up in the restored chalet behind the villa.

You'd never know that *Les Frênes*, as Turgenev called the property, was there. It's hidden nowadays up the hillside in a forest of fir, weeping willows and ash (the *frênes* of its name) behind some modern flats and a petrol station. Once inside the gate, however, you're magically in Russia, although how the magic works is a bit of a mystery.

The Viardots' villa, for instance, which gradually reveals itself through the trees as you climb the hill, is a small, white neo-classical building, symmetrical and restrained, with slender Greek columns around the entrance and on the balcony above it. In other words, it is exactly the sort of house many a wealthy Russian landowner would have built himself in the early nineteenth century – exactly the sort of house, in point of fact, that so much of *Virgin Soil* is set in. I don't know how the Viardots furnished the house when they moved into it, but the Sipyagins in *Virgin Soil* in the late 1860s decorated their drawing-room, 'heavy with the scent of lilies-of-the-valley', in 'the most up-to-date, refined' style: their cretonne upholstery and curtains were in 'pleasantly varied tints', while their 'china, bronze and cut-glass knick-knacks, scattered about on the shelves and tables, were all remarkable for the gentle sense of balance they blended together to create in the cheerful rays of May sunshine streaming in freely through the high, wide-open windows'. As Turgenev noted, it made for a 'delightful picture'. There were no cretonne curtains visible at the windows of the Viardot villa on this particular Sunday morning, if indeed they had ever hung there. In fact, the house had a closed-off, abandoned air that morning.

Turgenev's own house, which you first glimpse as you turn the corner of the villa and peer further up the hill into the firs to the right, is a miniature Swiss chalet, of all things! Nevertheless, somehow or other it manages to remind you of a Russian dacha. Is it the carved woodwork and gay colours (blue, pink and cream) which give it that slightly gingerbread look, still to be seen in some Russian villages today? Or is it simply the dreamy forest all around it, with its promise of shady nooks and sun-dappled glades, meandering paths and rough-hewn seats on which to court or read a book? Whatever it is, you can't help feeling that just around the next corner you'll happen upon a character or two from some Russian novel you've been reading: a young woman, perhaps, strolling along in a white dress and straw sun-hat, arm in arm with a quaintly dressed, quietly anguished young man, talking about poetry or the meaning of life.

'C'est beau,' Daniel murmured, looking around him with a kind of mild surprise, and indeed it was. The quiet, the green, the feathered light beneath the trees – it was all very beautiful. But his saying so reassured me a little. I'd been feeling apprehensive.

The reason for my apprehension was simple: I knew that Les Frênes would turn out to be what Russians call a 'dom-muzei'. Part shrine, part exhibition space, the typical Russian dom-muzei is a cleaned-up version of some famous person's house (that being the dom part), with memorabilia displayed in glass cases around the walls of certain rooms (that being the *muzei* part). Whenever I come across the word, I have a vision of stiff little rooms of period furniture, half cordoned-off and smelling of wax, with a guide reeling off information nobody needs or could possibly remember to a stony-faced crowd with its mind on tea and sandwiches. (*In September that same year, Ivan Ivanovich . . . The lampshades are exact replicas of . . . You'll notice on the second shelf from the top a Russian–Swedish dictionary. Now, when his daughter . . .*) I see an empty, immaculately made bed with a pitcher (empty of water) on the bed-side table; a silent, dust-free drawing-room dotted about with unsat-on chairs; a study with all the books lined up on shelves in locked cabinets; and in the nursery, instead of smelly cots, stained carpets and stray toys, I see under glass a row of fob-watches, pens, assorted photographs together with bills from the tailor and letters of no consequence (*Dear Stepan Stepanovich, How are you? And how's that lame dog of yours? Any better? If this foul weather clears by Tuesday, I may very well . . .*) What I see, in other words, is the mummification of a lived life – with relics.

In my time I have traipsed through countless *doma-muzei* all over Russia – and not only in Russia, but in France and England as well. We even have one or two of them in Tasmania. So I couldn't help feeling apprehensive about what I'd find at Bougival. It wouldn't be something I could imagine Daniel warming to at all. At the same time, I had to see it. I wanted to see with my own eyes what the words 'Les Frênes' and 'Bougival', so often met with in books about Turgenev, meant. In part, too, I think I felt drawn to it in order to pay my respects to a man whose voice had been talking to me in enriching ways for over half my life. After all, the strange house in front of us was where, in his upstairs bedroom at precisely 2 pm on 3rd September 1883, he had died. (The family had had to hurry back from lunch to be with him.) Like attending funerals, I suppose that paying our respects is something we feel impelled to do to affirm the great good somebody has brought into our lives. It needn't be at all the same thing as worshipping at a shrine.

So those two small syllables – *c'est beau* – banal, almost meaningless, gave me heart. They promised me a sympathetic companion while I paid my respects, as well as patience if I chose to linger with the mummy (as it were) for a little longer than he, Daniel, felt inclined to do.

———

Being a little early by arrangement, we were met at the door to the chalet by the almost legendary (at least in Russian literary circles) Alexandre Zviguilsky. This was the man who, together with his wife and son, had created the museum I was feeling such unease about. It was Dr Zviguilsky, with the Association of Friends that he and his family had formed, who had rescued the property from ruin and eventual demolition.

Given his almost fifty years of dedicated scholarship, the decades devoted to restoring the villa and the chalet, to organising concerts, exhibitions and symposia, to publishing books and specialist articles on Turgenev and the Viardots – given, in short, Alexandre Zviguilsky's overwhelming erudition and passion for Turgenev, I had been expecting somebody a little fiercer than he turned out to be.

The man in the elegant summer suit who ushered us inside had that particular mixture of charm, intensity of feeling and intellect that I imagine had struck so many people about Turgenev himself when they met him. Skipping lightly from French to Russian and back to

French – not always noticing, I suspect, which language he was speaking – he seemed happy, as Ivan Sergeyevich had been, to say a few considered words on any topic, from the weather to the names of trees, the perfidy of the St Cloud municipal council, which was threatening to close the museum down, or death itself. But the warmth in each remark, whether on weeping willows, wall coverings or the garden in *Virgin Soil*, came, I felt, from a single flame.

Beneath the apparent expansiveness, it seemed to me, there burnt a very singular passion.

This sort of all-consuming passion makes me feel both envious and slightly disconcerted. Whenever I sense it smouldering behind the screen of conversation, I can't help wondering if I've ever loved anything in my life with quite that kind of intimate knowledge and fidelity. I've certainly never managed to see anything I've loved so splendidly *incarnated* as Zviguilsky's love for Turgenev has been in *Les Frênes*. What joy there must be in that, as well as that element of fatigue and fettered toil which every great love (whether of gardens, Jesus, football, socialism or even one's own children) inevitably seems to entail.

ONE OF THE REASONS I am tempted to cast my conversation with Dr Zviguilsky in this light may be the sudden switch that morning in my attitude to Turgenev. It was nothing Dr Zviguilsky said. Nor was it any particular object in the house – not the original writing-desk, nor the piano; not even the bed he died in or Claudie Viardot's touching portrait of her mother in old age. Nor was there any specific moment of illumination. It was gradual. By the time I said goodbye to Dr Zviguilsky at the back door and set off to catch Daniel before he disappeared again, I simply thought of Turgenev rather differently. After all those years.

It didn't happen downstairs. Why would it? In the three downstairs rooms – the former kitchen (now a small vestibule), dining-room and music room – I found little trace of Turgenev. This was the strongly *muzei* part of the *dom-muzei*. Dr Zviguilsky would have been astounded, possibly even indignant, if he'd known that that's what I was thinking as I followed him about: every inch of these rooms, after all, is ostensibly covered with 'traces' of Ivan Sergeyevich Turgenev. Peering at the pictures of famous Russians Turgenev knew, I nodded and smiled and murmured '*Kak interesno!*' I looked at the old editions of his works, including a valuable first edition of *A Hunter's Notes* (I think) and (from memory) the first French translation of something or other of his, and said '*Incroyable! Fantastique!*' In the delightful music room, where concerts are still occasionally held, I politely marvelled at the piano brought from Baden-Baden – his fingers, and Pauline's, had touched these keys; perhaps even (who knows?) Liszt's or Saint-Saëns' or Brahms'. I respectfully studied letters in the great writer's own hand under glass around the wall. '*Ochen, ochen interesno . . .*' I said, bending over the yellowing pieces of paper, unable to think of another adjective. '*Ochen . . .*' ('Very').

In fact, I felt almost nothing at all. All these photographs and sketches of famous writers and artists, all these exhibits of letters and notes and books, gave me no sense of meeting Turgenev, and I was in no mood for a school excursion. I didn't want information, I wanted transcendence. I wanted to *hear his voice.*

My gaze kept wandering to the windows at the end of the room, giving onto a balcony surrounded by trees. I could imagine Turgenev leaving the windows open while he was reading or entertaining in order to catch the slightest sound of Pauline giving one of her classes in the severely beautiful stone house just down the hill, or the laughter of the young folk playing croquet in the sun.

But somehow that wasn't enough.

Daniel, on the other hand, seemed quite engrossed in all these objects. Hearing a voice was not yet something he needed to do. When Dr Zviguilsky and I went upstairs, he was still happily reading the letters under glass, getting his bearings.

It was at the top of the staircase that I first felt moved. Stepping into his study, with its rich, red wall-coverings and wide view downhill towards the river, I felt something shift in my attitude towards Turgenev, the way it does when somebody you know well will sometimes tell a joke or comment on a film they've seen and all of a sudden, to your surprise, you find yourself looking at this old friend quite differently.

The desk is there – his *actual* desk, the desk he really once sat at, finishing off *Virgin Soil*, and dreaming up 'Klara Milich', 'Song of Triumphant Love' and one or two other dark, yet glittering, fantastic tales from his last years. Ivan Sergeyevich Turgenev once sat at this very table, slitting open letters from Russia and scribbling notes to friends all over Europe. It's tiny.

Right behind the desk is his massive bookcase, a work of art in heavy, black wood. He'd often have swivelled on his solid black-wood chair to take a book from its shelves – it could have been in Russian, French, English, German, Italian, Spanish or even some more exotic language – searching for inspiration. The chair is there, too, covered in gleaming red morocco. The bookcase and chair are replicas, it's true, part of the Zviguilskys' painstaking restoration of the upstairs rooms, but they have to be there if you want to imagine yourself in Ivan Sergeyevich's shoes, if you want to be catapulted back. Oddly enough, the very *thinginess* of the objects in the room – I touched the woven Venetian red wall-covering, the warm wood of the desk – lend the room an extraordinary transparency. This time when I said '*C'est fantastique!*' I meant it.

It's a wonderfully large, light room, with windows on three sides (the chalet is only one room deep), and it's no wonder that blue-eyed Claudie, his favourite amongst the Viardot children (for reasons the rumour-mongers were happy to suggest), used to set up her easel here in its western corner and paint. It was still standing there that morning, with several portraits of her mother on display around it. How beautiful Pauline Viardot became in grey-haired old age, by the way, at least in her daughter's eyes. (She died almost twenty-seven years after Turgenev and her husband.) It was surprisingly easy to imagine the family gatherings in that room of an afternoon after Pauline's last class had finished, when they'd all troop up the hill to see 'Tourgel': Claudie would be painting, Pauline laying aside her needlework to talk to one of her grandchildren, while Louise (the eldest daughter – and Ivan Sergeyevich's least favourite) read aloud from some freshly arrived book (an English novel, perhaps, or one of Maupassant's stories). Sometimes they would play charades or forfeits, or even all clatter downstairs to the drawing-room to stand around the piano and sing. As often as not Tourgel would make a nuisance of himself by slurping his tea, interrupting the reading with exclamations of 'That reminds me! I once met a man . . .' and commenting on Claudie's progress at the easel.

Nobody has to stand in that room in Bougival, obviously, in order to imagine this scene. There are books and internet sites in several languages which describe it all in detail with coloured illustrations. What dissolved the old image of Turgenev in my mind was not just the experience of standing there on the parquetry he had had installed, conjuring up a scene from his life. It had nothing to do with thinking to myself: 'Ah! So that's the inkwell he dipped his pen in!' It was a matter of feeling, for the first time in my journey in Turgenev's footsteps, the homeliness of his connection with the space I was standing in. This was where he'd finally woven his true nest. This room, even more than the flat in the rue de Douai, was the embodiment of the nest he'd longed for all his life. (No wonder he gave this property the name of a tree.) And in this room the intimacy of the concerns that actually gave life to his large heart was palpable.

Almost anyone who began reading Turgenev or about Turgenev during the Soviet era, as I did, would almost certainly have built up a picture with a different colouring. According to this picture Turgenev was primarily a writer and thinker at the epicentre of social change in Russia. Did not the tsar himself acknowledge Turgenev's role in the abolition of serfdom? After reading *A Hunter's Notes*, with its cast of fully rounded peasant characters, Alexander is said to have grasped for the first time the inhumanity of the slave-owning system. Was it not Turgenev who drew the world's first portrait of a bolshevik in *Fathers and Sons,* decades before the word was coined? Did he not practically invent nihilism? Yes, he wrote well, or at least beautifully, but he excited our interest because of the way in which he charted nineteenth-century intellectual and social movements in Russia – idealism, revolutionary materialism, populism, every significant ideological shift in Russian social thought over three decades. He knew Bakunin, Herzen, Belinsky, Dostoyevsky and Tolstoy personally. He was a man 'profoundly and painfully concerned', as Isaiah Berlin has expressed it, 'with his country's condition and destiny'.

This picture is not a false one, either. However, upstairs at Bougival it dawns on you that it's skewed. Or, if not skewed, then one-sided. That all seemed to me now like shadow-play, not the candle itself; his shell, not his quick.

———

In *Russian Thinkers* Isaiah Berlin complains that 'most of [Turgenev's] readers' fail to appreciate what is truly great about him. In their ignorance, he says, they hold to the idea of Turgenev as no more than 'the writer of beautiful lyrical prose, the author of nostalgic idylls of country life, the elegiac poet of the last enchantments of decaying country houses and of their ineffective but irresistibly attractive inhabitants, the incomparable story-teller with a marvellous gift for describing nuances of mood and feeling, the poetry of nature and of love . . .'

Precisely who thinks of Turgenev in this equally skewed way, Berlin does not say. (Virginia Woolf, as I mentioned, scotched the myth of the 'incomparable story-teller' well over half a century ago.) Berlin confines himself to referring vaguely to the views of Henry James, the Anglo-Irish writer George Moore, the largely forgotten critic and novelist Maurice Baring and 'French memoirs of the time'.

To be frank, these are not views I have often encountered. Certainly, I can find no trace of them in Henry James' celebrated essay on Turgenev. On the contrary, James takes pains to emphasise the point that, while Turgenev wrote fiction and plays, 'the great drama of his life was the struggle for a better state of things in Russia. In this drama he played a most distinguished part . . .' James claimed that Turgenev talked 'almost exclusively about Russia' whenever they met, while his aim in his work was always to 'show us life itself', regardless of the effect this had on the elegance of the storytelling. I also wonder precisely which 'critics on the right and on the left', as he puts it, Berlin considered responsible for the misleading 'conventional picture of Turgenev as a pure artist drawn into political strife against his will while remaining fundamentally alien to it'. He does not name them. 'Against his will' – possibly, but 'pure'? Who has ever said that?

In that rich red upstairs study all the different Turgenevs I had come across – political thinker, elegiac poet, 'incomparable story-teller' – began to come together in a new configuration. The 'sweet-natured giant' of Edmond de Goncourt's reminiscences, the medieval trouba-dour trembling at the feet of the finest and gentlest lady in the world, Tom Stoppard's pessimistic liberal tossing off witty Stoppardesque one-liners, chronicler of the Russian intelligentsia's development, entrancing conversationalist, exile, realist, romantic, rhapsodist of unrequited love, dabbler in the paranormal, buffoon, hunter, Hamlet, Don Quixote – they all began to shake down into a single, intricate pattern. As in Dr Zviguilsky's conversation (or Daniel the Buddhist's, for that matter – perhaps even mine), the effervescence of colours, shapes and themes in Turgenev's life and works now appeared to me to have been produced by a single hidden flame. If I had to give this flame a name, I'd call it mortal love. All these Turgenevs, whatever they said or did, now appeared to me to be variations on this single theme, refractions of a single flame: I love you, yet we must die.

At the desk beside me, dipping his pen into the very inkwell my eyes were resting on, Turgenev wrote barely a syllable of social history, apart from certain passages in *Virgin Soil*. Like the scenes Renoir and Monet were painting at the bottom of his garden, although in much more sombre tones, the pictures he painted in this room in his stories and his poems in prose had virtually no connection at all with the intellectual currents of the time. Nor had his writing had any political colouring, in any vital sense, since the wounding fiasco of *Fathers and Sons* well over a decade before he settled in Bougival. What he wrote about at this desk was love and death. Love which alone makes sense of being alive, yet is snuffed out in death. (Or is it?) Love which makes the thought of death unbearable, yet alone can take away its sting. (How?) Love and death. Nothing else.

When he told his friend Countess Lambert, after the flare-up over *Fathers and Sons*, that he had never been interested in politics and never would be, in one sense he was telling the truth. 'I pay attention to politics,' he told her, 'only in so far as a writer called upon to depict contemporary life must.' Exactly.

In fact, it is even tempting to suggest that the role his *Hunter's Notes* played, with its cast of fully rounded peasant characters, in convincing the tsar that serfdom must be abolished may have been largely accidental. Certainly, the unsentimental picture he painted of peasants as human beings as complex and worthy of respect as their social betters was refreshing, but he may well have been simply describing hunting scenes which feudal landlords had taken for granted for centuries but which no writer had thought to describe truthfully before. Oxford University, in awarding him an honorary doctorate for his part in emancipating the peasants, took a more generous view.

'BUT WHAT ABOUT *VIRGIN SOIL*? I thought you said he wrote that here,' Daniel said when I tried to explain to him what I felt I'd *seen through to* in the study. We were on the N13 at the time, headed back into Paris. 'As far as I can see, the whole novel's about this bunch of city intellectuals trying to stir up revolt amongst the peasants.' (Daniel, I'd noticed, had found the bedroom and study much less interesting than the museum on the ground floor. Upstairs it was he who had mostly stood at the window musing on the garden before disappearing down the stairs again.)

'You see, I don't think that's what *Virgin Soil* is about at all,' I said, which I dare say mildly annoyed him, 'any more than *Harry Potter* is about wizards.'

'I haven't read *Harry Potter*.'

'Well, any more than *The Boating Party* . . . you know, the Renoir . . .'

'Yes, I know the Renoir.'

'. . . is about . . . boating parties, or boats, or parties.'

'What do you think it's about?'

'Colour, I suppose. And possibly pleasure. But not boats or parties.'

'So what, *cher maître*, do you think *Virgin Soil* is about?'

'It's about what it's possible to believe in, given death, if you've had an education. And the answer is: nothing at all, unless you were born with a believing nature. That's what the novel's *about*.'

And I meant it. It's a very dark novel, for all the 'beautiful lyrical prose', to borrow Isaiah Berlin's wording, the 'irresistibly attractive inhabitants' of country houses, the 'nuances of mood and feeling, the poetry of nature and of love'. And it's a novel utterly of our time, I now realise. (It's taken me thirty years.)

The reason Turgenev's novels, even *Virgin Soil*, are all so much of our time and still so heart-breaking to read is (again in Virginia Woolf's words) that Turgenev speaks 'not as a prophet clothed in thunder but a seer who tries to understand'. The melancholy that imbues them is the melancholy of the observer who, unlike Gogol, Dostoyevsky or Tolstoy, has no brightly-hued scenario to replace his mournful vision with.

'Well, in the introduction to my edition,' Daniel said when I explained all this, 'it says that the novel was extremely prophetic. Wasn't there a trial in Moscow, just a month after the book came out . . . ?'

'Yes, yes, I know. And everyone said that the revolutionaries were so like the ones in *Virgin Soil* that Turgenev must have been part of the plot! But that's not the point . . . Yes, he was a brilliant observer – he knew young people like these, both in Russia and here in Paris – they used to scrounge money off him; he knew how they talked and cut their hair and what blouses and boots they wore; he knew the men who'd inspired them – Bakunin, Belinsky and Herzen and so on were his friends . . . He'd been thinking about how to bring about change in Russia before most of these young plotters were born.'

'*But that's not the point.*' Daniel was mocking me, taking off my accent. 'So what is the point?'

It wasn't easy to argue my case, but I believed that Virginia Woolf was essentially right about Turgenev. What the seer tries to understand in *Virgin Soil*, I said, thinking aloud, is not the historical details of the failed attempts of high-minded radicals to foment revolution amongst the peasants in the late 1860s, but how it is impossible to believe in anything – even a cause as just as revolution – or to sacrifice yourself to that cause, when you don't believe in yourself (don't love yourself), when you see yourself as nothing but a pinprick of mould on a grain of sand, about to be dead forever, just a biochemical reaction in a brain, as we might say nowadays. Commentators can argue endlessly over whether or not the radicals in *Virgin Soil* are Bakuninists or Blanquists or unhistorical fabrications, but such cogitations are beside the point: they are just the scenery for a play about the complete breakdown of any rationale for acting (or loving) in an utterly senseless world.

———

Some people manage to believe, of course. Some seem born to it, programmed from birth to give themselves to higher causes, everything from church fêtes to the Revolution. Yet others are ready to believe in anything at all, as we know from catching the occasional televangelist beamed in from Tennessee. Some are so fired up for action by requited love that they can't stop looking for ways to love even more widely – loving Marianna or Alexei makes them want to love the whole world. Yet others, having no Marianna or Alexei to love, love humanity, ideas, ideals and radiant futures instead with a burning passion. All these types make their appearance in *Virgin Soil*, plodding around the villages and hamlets of S— province, sleeping in haylofts and cowsheds, haranguing peasants and workers in taverns and workmen's barracks, teaching, preaching, handing out pamphlets and running from the police.

The 'character at the centre' of the novel, from whom Woolf's 'succession of emotions' radiates, Alexei Nezhdanov, the handsome, pale-faced, chestnut-haired representative of the younger generation, ultimately proves too acutely aware of his own nothingness to love himself, any of the women who fall under his spell or the revolution. For a time, like all the true believers in his clandestine group, he too shouts slogans at passing peasants ('Rise up! Down with taxes! Down with the landowners!' – that sort of thing). As one critic has put it, he behaves for a time like a Hamlet hurtling hysterically into quixotry. But when he goes home to bed in the charming neoclassical manor with the cretonne curtains where he's tutoring the landowner's son for the summer, it's not the brutalised, starving peasants he's spent the day with that he thinks about (any more than Turgenev thought about the brutalised working class in France). What he thinks about (like Turgenev) is 'the inevitable end, death . . . annihilation'.

Eventually he tells his fellow revolutionary and fiancée Marianna, with whom he has eloped from the charming neoclassical house, 'I don't believe any more in the cause which brought us together, for which we ran away from that house together . . . I don't believe in it! I don't believe in it! . . . I used to think I believed in the cause itself, only doubting myself, my own strength, my own abilities . . . But these two things obviously can't be separated – what's the point of deceiving myself? No, I don't even believe in the cause.' And so he kills himself. And that's the end.

'WERE YOU SURPRISED BY HIS SUICIDE?' I asked Daniel later as we inched our way towards the Marais in one of those interminable Parisian traffic-jams. (It had taken us a lot longer than three-quarters of an hour to get back to town.) He didn't say anything at first. He just looked out at the back of the car in front of us and thrummed on the driving-wheel. 'Disappointed? Annoyed? Outraged? Disgusted?' I was asking because people often are.

In his green bedroom at Bougival, across the landing from his study, when he lay dying in great pain, Turgenev begged visitors to give him poison. In the rue de Douai, where his cries of agony could be heard up and down the street, he implored his infinitely loved Pauline to throw him from the window. (She told him he was far too big and heavy – and he laughed.) He asked Guy de Maupassant, right at the end, to give him a revolver. This is something we can all understand. A man clearly at the very end of his days, in appalling pain – there is nothing there to surprise or annoy or disgust any of us. In a rush of tenderness many of us would even agree to help bring the suffering to an end.

There are other kinds of suicide as well which, unlikely as we might be to assist in them, we can at least understand. As we know, there are some kinds of anguish which seem both unbearable and certain to be never-ending when they first engulf the sufferer. Desperate for oblivion, the abandoned lover, the bereft widow, the shamed family man, can easily end up courting the idea of death.

Turgenev wrote about this kind of suicide, too, more than once. In 'Klara Milich', for instance, one of the last stories he ever wrote (there in his study at Bougival), a moody actress, a 'gypsy' (swarthy, passionate, with dark, tragic eyes) fastens all her hopes for a beautiful life on a rather unprepossessing and awkward, not to say consumptive, young admirer in the front row at one of her recitals. Spurned, like Pushkin's Tatyana, when she makes a rather gauche advance towards him, she becomes despondent, decides that she will never be able to live as she wants, yet can't keep living the way she is, and so poisons herself. Strange to relate, once she is dead, the love affair blossoms (if 'love' is the right word for this kind of obsession) – or so the young man seems to believe, as he sinks into delirium, rending the night air with his wild, ecstatic cries of love triumphant. In 'Klara Milich' Turgenev actually handles all this Romantic palaver with surprising panache. Even the rationally minded Russian intelligentsia admired it greatly.

A second-rate provincial actress with no prospects is one thing, but Nezhdanov? A clever, well-connected young man from the capital, strikingly good-looking, sensitive, creative (he writes poetry), with every prospect of leading an interesting, useful life . . . why would a man like this commit suicide? He wasn't ill or in pain, he was in no serious danger, he was loved – in fact, almost every woman who crossed his path was smitten with him – why would he want to die? What was unbearable about his life? The starving peasants in their pestilential mud huts didn't kill themselves, the workers slaving in filthy, dangerous factories for a pittance didn't kill themselves, nor did convicts in chain-gangs in Siberia, flogged, worked to death, fed on gruel and separated for years from their loved ones. But the soft-skinned poet Nezhdanov did at twenty-two.

'No, I wasn't surprised,' Daniel said eventually. 'Or annoyed or disgusted.' He smiled. We were edging forwards steadily now, if slowly. 'I think I understand him all too well. Whenever I've felt like killing myself – and I used to all the time once, strange as it may seem, I used to just wait for the right day to do it, the day when it would cause least fuss – it was never because anything was wrong. When I broke up with . . .'

'Yes, I remember.' (It had been dreadful.)

'. . . or when I got the diagnosis . . . no, those were never the times. What made me want to stop living was the feeling that hope was pointless. And I could feel that in the metro, at home on the sofa watching television . . . anywhere, really, at any time.' Wormwood, I thought to myself. He's tasted the wormwood.

'Hope of what?'

'Hope,' he said after a pause, 'that it could ever add up to anything beautiful.'

'What?'

'This mess.' And he waved out the window at one of the most overwhelmingly beautiful streets in the world. But I knew what he meant. 'Indifference – that's what was unbearable. The world's, my own . . . The only thing that ever helped,' he went on with a bemused chuckle, 'was music.' Now that was something Turgenev would have understood perfectly.

As well as music, Daniel now, of course, has religion, although not God, since he's a Buddhist – at least, not God as such. The universe for Daniel is no longer everything. He is an apprentice magician. Once or twice I've felt myself slipping under his spell. He rarely refers to it directly any more, but that's the little flame that burns away under the surface of any conversation with him. It's the candle lighting the shadow-play called *Life with Daniel*.

Religion left Turgenev cold – or at least all the paraphernalia of doctrine and ritual did, while the Orthodox God struck him as about as lovable as a thunderstorm – and just as pitiless and unpredictable. Not even as a child or adolescent did it appeal to him – not surprisingly, since his mother, like so many of the Russian gentry, had little time for the superstitions of the common folk.

It's worth remembering that there was not even a modern Russian translation of the complete Bible to study until 1876 – Herzen read the New Testament in German. So Orthodox beliefs must have appeared to the young Ivan as more a collection of folklore than a metaphysical system he should take seriously. Yet in his maturity he didn't reject religion stridently, as many in his circle did, including Louis Viardot (Pauline, while free-thinking, never succumbed to atheism); nor did he seek to trump arguments for God's existence with scientific arguments against it.

In his voluminous correspondence with his close friend Countess Lambert, an ardent believer in Russian Orthodoxy, Ivan Sergeyevich always sounded more regretful than argumentative. On the whole, religion (and in particular Orthodoxy and Catholicism) seems simply to have failed to hold his attention. I feel much the same way about astrophysics and sport, for example, although I know that for millions of human beings the cosmos revolves around these things. 'God', or at least the Orthodox Christian god, was not the answer to any question Turgenev was interested in putting.

He was aware, however, as he wrote to Countess Lambert that 'whoever has [religious] faith has all there is to have and can lose nothing, while whoever has no faith has nothing'. In need of consolation (as we all are), he kept close watch all his life for something to have faith in, some sign that he might not after all lose *everything* in dying, particularly during those last years in Paris and at *Les Frênes*, when he often found himself ill and in pain.

In this day and age it is difficult to take too seriously the kind of supernatural hocus-pocus and emanations from the afterworld which so many of his stories seem to hinge on in the final years – all the prophetic dreams, black magic, telepathy, messages from the dead, phantoms, disembodied voices and visions. Nowadays, although many of these stories are still quite chilling, they are almost unreadable. Even Turgenev used phrases like 'a complete fiasco' and 'absolute nonsense' to describe a couple of them.

At the time, though, in the atmosphere reigning in educated circles right across Europe in the 1870s, occult phenomena were widely held to be well worth investigating for signs of selves or souls not contingent on bodies for their existence or survival. As early as the 1860s in Russia, almost as a complement to the drift into scientism, the fad for spiritualist séances, table-turning and automatic writing had been growing apace. Even the tsar had been impressed by Douglas Dunglas Home's demonstrations of his levitation skills: he rose right up to the ceiling at Peterhof in 1858. (Turgenev had also witnessed Home's antics in Paris the year before, but had been less impressed than the tsar.) These phenomena offered hope – as they still do to many – of a continuing presence in a parallel dimension not annihilated by earthly decay or death and therefore of undying love. Untouched by any hint of spiritual perception, they nonetheless hinted that the universe might turn out to be a much queerer and more fantastic place than common notions of what was natural and supernatural might allow. They cocked a snook at the universe of blind chance.

There was more to it than that, though. Turgenev was no mere parlour spiritualist, hoping for an eternity of days with his beloved simply because . . . well, simply because he couldn't conceive of living without her. In fact, it's living *with* anybody for all eternity that it's virtually impossible for any of us to conceive of, let alone with Pauline Viardot or one of Turgenev's slightly stony virgins. The mind shuts down, all we can picture is more of the same – a kind of endless Sunday afternoon. Dante's vision of measureless movement (whirling, winding, enfolding, embracing, burning, comprehending) in a Divine Mind where there is no 'where' (as he put it) is beyond most of us, fixated as we are on objects in space.

What Turgenev ultimately wanted, I think, was to be able to believe that something existed beyond time, beyond the sluggish, empty day-after-day-ness of his lived life. When we cut through all the premonitions, levitations and meetings with the devil, it becomes apparent that it was *time* that he was locked in battle with in his supernatural tales, resorting, naturally enough, to the weapons at his disposal. In his case they came from a Romantic armoury. As far as we can tell he lost the battle.

Born at a time when most people still believed in some sort of three-tiered universe – there was the supernatural world, the natural and, at some remove, there were human beings – he had lived on into an era when there was only indifferent nature left, which is more or less where we find ourselves stranded today. Everything else, as he wrote in the summer of 1879 (here, no doubt, at Bougival) – 'people', 'good', 'mind', 'justice' – was just words. Outside the natural universe there was nothing. We pray unreasonably that this might not be so, but all prayer, he wrote two years before he died, was essentially a desperate appeal to God to make two plus two not equal four. But it did, his reason told him, and always would. And so he spent the last two decades of his life 'in a sort of misty, painful vacuum' between hope and reason.

Painful it might have been, but it's actually a fruitful terrain for any artist to inhabit, so long as he doesn't become self-pitying. Now and again – not often, but in some of his *Poems in Prose*, for example – Turgenev did verge on self-pity. There's an almost voluptuous edge to the courting of his pain in some of his letters and other writings, which is not attractive.

IN THE GREEN BEDROOM where Turgenev died that September afternoon in 1883, across the landing from the red study, I found no trace at
all of the last terrible months – the agonising trips back and forth to
Paris, the death of his friend Louis Viardot a few months before his
own, Pauline's grief as her intimate friend of forty years drifted away
into drugged dreams and then silence, the droves of distraught Russian
visitors. There was no hint of the desperate attempts to fend off death
with miracle cures, such as the one involving drinking two dozen glasses
of milk a day (which did indeed make him feel a lot better for a time).

The feeling I had when I walked into that room was more of Ivan
Sergeyevich having just stepped out for an hour or two – perhaps to
pay the Viardots a visit or to take a stroll with a friend in the woods
behind the house. Had the maid just come in to make the bed and tidy
the room? Somebody had put fresh flowers in a vase and opened the
doors onto the balcony to let the breezes in. Out on the balcony I
caught the scent of damp leaves and woodsmoke. I half expected to
hear his high-pitched voice growing louder as he made his way up the

hill towards me. The intimacy of those upstairs rooms made it hard to believe that he was not close by. It concertina'd time.

It was in this room, however, that he must have discovered the answer to the question he'd asked himself four years before in those same somewhat maudlin *Poems in Prose*: 'What will I be thinking when it comes time to die, if I'm able to think at all?' Would he be thinking about how he'd wasted so much of his life, 'slept through it', not knowing how to partake of its gifts? Would he be horrified, he wondered, by the suddenness of his end and think in panic of all the things he'd been intending to do? Would he dwell on happy moments, faces, scenes from his past? Remember his sins and repent of them? Would he try to imagine what, if anything, was awaiting him beyond the grave? 'No,' he wrote, 'I think I'll be trying not to think at all – occupying my mind with all sorts of silly nonsense so as to distract myself from the threatening dark, the blackness ahead.'

In fact, for the record, if those who were with him in that green bedroom on the last two days are to be believed, what was uppermost in his mind at the end was finding a way, as words began to fail him, of assuring those he loved of the depth and reality of his love for their goodness. What is love if not joy in another's goodness? He seemed to want not to leave them but to melt into them.

It was in this room, I like to think, propped up in the green bed in front of me, that Turgenev, mortal love incarnate, wrote:

> When I am no more, when everything I once was has
> crumbled into dust – oh you, my only friend, you whom I
> loved so deeply and tenderly, you who will surely survive
> me – do not go to my grave . . . There is nothing for you to
> do there.

Do not forget me . . . but do not remember me in the midst of your daily cares, pleasures and needs . . . I don't want to interfere with your life, to trouble its calm flow. But, at times of solitude, when that shy sadness, unprovoked and so well-known to kind hearts, comes over you, take one of our favourite books and find in it those pages, those lines, those words which used to make us both all at once – do you remember? – shed sweet, silent tears together.

Read, close your eyes, and stretch out your hand to me . . . Stretch out your hand to your absent friend.

I will not be able to press your hand in mine: mine will be lying motionless beneath the earth. But I feel joyful now to think that you will perhaps feel something lightly touching your hand.

And my image will rise up before you, and from beneath your closed eyelids will flow tears like the tears which the two of us, moved by Beauty, once shed together, oh my only friend, whom I loved so deeply and so tenderly.

———

For quite a long time I stood on the bedroom balcony, contemplating the sunlit Russian forest all around me, and felt alive to the man dying in the bed behind me. When I turned to say a word or two (I hardly knew which ones) to my companions, I found I was completely alone. In the blink of an eye both my guide and Daniel seemed to have abracadabra'd themselves into thin air. What bliss! At that moment, if I'd known how to, I'd have cast some spell and evaporated without a word to anybody as well. As it was, I hung there, like a droplet in the air, neither borne aloft nor plummeting to the ground. Then, a few minutes, or possibly half an hour or more later, where the Viardot villa stood with its back to me, like a stage-set – white, flat, lifeless, shutters closed, slightly sinister – I caught sight of Daniel's red windcheater glowing in the sun on the tiny terrace and I floated slowly down to earth.

Some time soon, I thought to myself on the way downstairs to say goodbye to Dr Zviguilsky, I really should go back to Russia, something I had been putting off doing for a long time, afraid that *my* Russia, the Russia under whose spell I had fallen almost a whole lifetime before, would no longer be there. I feared I might 'go home', as it were, and find the house empty. Perhaps the thing to do would be to 'go home' to a place I could be sure would not be empty – to Spasskoye, Turgenev's childhood home, the house he wrote his greatest books in, returning there from St Petersburg, Berlin, Baden-Baden and Paris over and over again until two years before he died. I had never actually been there, although, in an odd kind of way, I'd thought of Spasskoye for years as where I came from.

PART THREE

RUSSIA

———

Russia! Russia! I can see you now, from my wondrous,
beautiful afar I can see you. How poor, how straggling,
how comfortless you are . . . But what is the
unfathomable, mysterious power that draws me to you?
Why can I hear your mournful song resounding
ceaselessly in my ears . . . ? What is it about this song?
What is it that calls and sobs and clutches at my
heart? . . . Russia! What do you want of me? What is the
unfathomable bond lying mysteriously hidden between
us? . . . Russia, are you not like a brisk troika nothing
can overtake? . . . Russia! Where are you flying off to?
Answer me! She gives no answer. Her bells ring out with
a wondrous sound, the riven air roars and turns into
shreds of wind; everything on earth flies by, and, looking
askance, other nations and states stand aside and make
way for her.

NIKOLAI GOGOL, *DEAD SOULS*

WHAT EVERYONE HAD SAID TO ME (old Moscow hands, old friends from my student days) when they'd first heard I was off to Moscow after so many years was: 'You won't be able to believe your eyes, it's all completely changed.'

I'd barely stepped off the Red Arrow from St Petersburg before the questions starting coming: 'Well, what do you think? Isn't it amazing?' I knew I was supposed to say: 'It's astounding! It's all so different!' But all I felt when I first arrived was dazed. The city that had stood still for most of my life had suddenly taken off like an express train, leaving me stranded in the middle of nowhere.

McDonald's! Coca-Cola! Gucci! A gigantic Hugo Boss banner strung up where once . . . 'Look at that! Hugo Boss! Can you believe it? Remember the old Party banners everywhere?' *Yes, I remember:* GLORY TO THE SOVIET UNION! THE PEOPLE AND THE PARTY ARE UNITED! 'Cappuccino? Espresso? What do you feel like?' *Amazing – even the waiters are polite. And at the market on Saturday morning there's fresh fruit piled halfway to the ceiling, mountains of caviar, legs of Australian lamb.* 'Is that the Pirosmani? Can I book a table for four for tonight – say, around seven? By the window? *Spasibo! Do svidaniya!* (Can you believe it? Do you remember the pitched battle to get into any restaurant in Moscow worth eating at? The Praga – remember the Praga? Or the Aragvi? [*Laughter.*])' *Yes, I remember well. And once you'd bribed the doorman and got inside, frozen stiff, half the menu would be off.* 'Remember the public swimming-pool that used to be just over there? Stalin had knocked down Christ the Saviour and put in a swimming-pool, remember?' *And now Christ the Saviour's back again. Freshly gilded domes. Freshly gilded domes all over Moscow, for that matter. Nuns in the monastery gardens across from the Pirosmani. Christian bookshops. Jesus on television. Unbelievable.* 'Just look at this traffic! Worse than Paris.' *Whole traffic-jams of Mercedes-Benzes, gleaming new apartment blocks for the elite, automatic teller machines (dispensing US dollars, if you want them), getaway tours to Spain (dirt cheap), bowling alleys, internet cafés, half the street on the mobile phone. I can't believe my eyes.*

It's Pyongyang made over to look like Dallas.

———

When you flew into Moscow airport in the old days – way back in the sixties and seventies when I went there to study or visit friends – it was like arriving in fairyland. It was a slightly down-at-heel fairyland, admittedly, a Napoleonic fairyland ruled by a gang of wicked wizards, but a fairyland nonetheless. Just hours before, you'd been in London or Helsinki where everyone had agreed that the sky was blue, that two plus two made four and that the newspapers were full of lies. Here, starting at Sheremetyevo airport, people looked you straight in the eye and assured you that the sky was purple, two plus two made five and the newspapers told the truth. 'Without batting an eyelid,' I wrote to my father soon after arriving in 1966, 'they'll swear black and blue that Paris is the capital of Japan.' The textbooks were full of fairytales, too, television broadcast nothing but fairytales, the cinemas showed one fairytale after another and at the Bolshoi we were treated to *Giselle* and *Nutcracker Suite*. We were living in a make-believe kingdom of heaven on earth. It was exciting beyond belief.

It was also very Russian. Over a century earlier Turgenev's friend Belinsky had called Russia 'a phantom land', the truth about Russia (that it was an intellectual wasteland populated by slaves) being concealed under a crust of borrowed culture and an ocean of pious fictions. In my day it was no longer an intellectual wasteland, of course, but the truth about it was still hidden under a thick layer of myth and burnished lies, not all of them made up by Russians.

Although I was distressingly naive on my visits to Russia in the sixties and seventies – I hardly knew how to interpret the particular fantasia I was living in, had little idea where it had sprung from, and was blind to much of the beauty that was there – I knew perfectly well, as did my Russian friends, that the kingdom I was living in was built on chimeras. Not only was I aware of the barbed wire encircling us, the concentration camps, the endless butchering, the corruption and the shortages, I really did think about those things every morning when I first woke up and looked out across the city from my window high up on the Lenin Hills. Early on a winter's morning I would often wake to the sharp sound of women scraping at the ice on the dark street outside. Those thoughts and that cold, hard sound became one. But I always loved *being* in Moscow. To this day the smell of unleaded petrol makes me feel nostalgic.

THE EXCITEMENT I FELT at being in Moscow during the Soviet era is clear from my letters home to my father, especially during my first stay in the mid-sixties. For him, in his cottage by the sea in southern New South Wales, it must have been like getting letters from the moon. Almost every line of those weekly letters home, written on a Saturday afternoon as a rule, in my cramped third-floor room at the university, is aglow with the pleasure of finding myself living in this fabled land at last: the days spent in the salubrious silence of the Lenin Library; rocketing around from marble palace to marble palace on the phantasmagorical underground railway; all those gloves-off conversations about things that mattered urgently (and forever) over sharp-tasting soups, herring, stroganoff, caviar on fresh bread and glasses of tea – casting my mind back, I can almost smell the fug in those steamy kitchens and dining-rooms in winter. We went on trips to ancient towns like Pskov and Novgorod in the frost and snow, as remote from everything I knew as Timbuktu; there was an endless round of plays, ballet, opera, concerts, movies – not without a fight for tickets, but high culture was cheap and abundant in Moscow in those days.

As a young man from a town of no importance at the end of the world (a true 'town of N', as Gogol called such places) I felt like a prince at a never-ending ball. I don't even much complain in my letters about the months of sunlessness, the fog and slush and bitter cold – a few grumbles about the 'endless queues' (we queued for everything for hours a day – in cafeterias, restaurants, shops, cloakrooms, offices – in the villages I even saw old women queuing to use the water-pump), a few gripes about the 'general rudeness', a never-ending obsession with food – but that's all.

The blurred postcards of Moscow I sent my father at that time mostly show a Bauhaus fantasy (slightly tacky if you look too closely, like a tango palace the morning after) of sunlit tower-blocks on tree-lined streets dotted with busy, well-dressed pedestrians going about their perfectly normal lives. Quite often they would be going about their perfectly normal lives against a triumphal background of fountains, colonnades, statues and monuments. Somewhere in virtually every picture I sent him my father would also have glimpsed the turrets and spires of one of Moscow's Stalinist castles – in fact, I lived in one of them on the Lenin Hills – severely symmetrical fortresses, small cities, really, crammed into a single, soaring, Gothic fantasy. Even this time, whenever I passed one of these bizarre structures, Dostoyevsky's 'common, harmonious anthill, beyond all questioning' from *The Brothers Karamazov* popped into my head.

Everyday reality for most of those who lived there then was soul-crushing, the Bauhaus dream just the shell of a lifetime of drudgery tinged with fear, but being there for me was as thrilling as time-travel or waking up on the moon. Akhmatova, I remember, once said that she was 'happy' to have lived when she did (through the two World Wars, the Revolution, the famine, the terror, the murder of many she loved, the slaughter of tens of millions of her fellow citizens). 'I am happy,' she said, 'that I saw events which cannot be equalled.' On almost anyone else's lips these words would be incomprehensible, if not an outrage. I think I have some small inkling of what she meant (although not, of course, of what she felt).

Even on later visits – even in 1993 when I was caught up in the frightening putsch against Yeltsin, and the grim reality beneath the fairytale was erupting like an ugly rash on the surface – I enjoyed being there. It was harder to *love* being there by then, but only because it was harder to know any more where 'there' was. When I took the escalator up to the street at Oktyabrskaya metro station one Sunday afternoon in early October 1993 and was disgorged into a seething mob of anti-Yeltsin demonstrators battling the police, I thought for a moment that I'd surfaced by mistake in Paris or Rome. When I finally got back to the apartment and heard that further up the street I was living on the mob was now hacking bystanders to death, I felt I must be hallucinating. Moscow had turned into Lima or Caracas.

That night on television we watched the news broadcasts from Ostankino where the anti-Yeltsin mobs were working their way up the tower from studio to studio in the midst of a terrifying firefight, killing the broadcasters off floor by floor. One by one the stations went off the air. Between news flashes read by men about to die we were treated to advertisements for Mars Bars, cartoon comedies and an inane American horror movie about a rampaging virus. Twiddling the dial on the radio we got rock music and ads for detergents.

Even the next day, with Yeltsin's tanks surrounding parliament, blasting away at the upper storeys, I couldn't help feeling that what I was looking at was not Moscow at all, but some figment of my imagination.

There were still snipers on the streets and gunfire was echoing around the city, but the pavement kiosks were open, selling snacks and concert tickets, people were walking their dogs past tanks, young couples were eating their lunch on benches in the sun, crowds of shoppers were streaming in and out of the shops, stocking up for the week – even the smart perfumery on Tverskaya, I recall, was full of women dressed to kill, taking their time about choosing just the right French fragrance for their purposes. The next night I went with friends to the theatre to see an outrageously camp cabaret version of *The Maids*. The audience went wild with excitement. Was the blood on the streets outside just tomato sauce? Were the tanks made of cardboard? Or was I in Paraguay? Wherever I was, I wrote in my diary the following morning before leaving for the airport: 'I am sorry to be leaving.'

In fact, I could only have been in Russia. How could I have mistaken it for anything else? The basic script for what was unfolding had been written by Dostoyevsky over a century earlier in *The Brothers Karamazov*, not long before Turgenev died. It was a warning to Russia about what would happen if she abandoned true Christianity for socialism or Catholicism (varieties of the same big lie, from his point of view). Dostoyevsky infuriates me as a stylist, a thinker and a man, most of what he wrote reads like a report from a lunatic-asylum. Nevertheless, just as lunatics will sometimes turn to you (my mother did it, I remember, in her last days), look you straight in the eye and cut you to the quick with truths nobody else would have dared to voice, so on occasion Dostoyevsky can stun you with the brilliance of his prophetic insights.

In the tale of the Grand Inquisitor in this novel – a tale which Ivan Karamazov makes up and tells his brother – the sixteenth-century Spanish Inquisitor, Cardinal of Seville, is dismayed to find Jesus Christ wandering around the city, a smile of infinite compassion on his lips, healing the sick and raising the dead. Before he can do too much damage, the Cardinal has him seized and thrown into prison, intending to have him burnt at the stake the following day as a heretic. In my day, Brezhnev would no doubt have dealt with Karl Marx with the same alacrity, if he'd turned up on Red Square babbling about workers throwing off their chains.

Now, the old Cardinal is no fool. He doesn't even believe in God. As he explains to Jesus, when he goes to visit him in his cell, freedom is a nice idea, and he appreciates Jesus' good intentions in wanting to bring people the freedom to choose good over evil, but in reality the herd can't cope with freedom, being by nature 'weak, depraved, worthless and rebellious'. Consequently, the herd's only chance of happiness lies in slavery. That way it will at least get bread. 'Enslave us, if that's how it must be,' the rabble cries, 'but feed us!'

Regrettably, as the Cardinal sees it, in this world that is indeed how it must be. For the rabble it will always be a choice between the two: bread and miracles on the one hand, freedom on the other. Given the choice, the Cardinal tells Jesus, the rabble will always opt for bread and miracles (presumably fake, since the Cardinal is an atheist) because even the mindless hordes know that, if left to their own devices, they would be too greedy to make certain that everyone got his rightful share of the bread. The Cardinal, having the Sword of Caesar in his hand, is in a position to give them what they would choose if they could. While he preens himself on having 'vanquished freedom' in order to make men happy, Jesus says nothing.

In Russia in the sixties and seventies we, too, had bread and miracles. We had to queue for the bread, it was sometimes in short supply and not always very appetising, but we did have it, and every morning in the underground on my way to the library, reading *Pravda*, I perused accounts of miracles far more wondrous than anything Jesus ever came up with, even the loaves and fishes or raising Lazarus. Rebellious heads were lopped off by the Sword of Caesar, certainly – in conversations around friends' kitchen tables or on walks along ill-lit streets where nobody could overhear us, I heard about what happened to those who spoke up for the freedom option – but I'm not sure that the herd was much troubled by this sort of culling. What the herd wanted first and foremost, and still does, and not only in Russia, was more bread (washing-machines, refrigerators, shoes, shampoos, and nowadays microwaves, DVDs and foreign cars). They may not have much liked the Grand Inquisitor, but they put their faith in him.

The Inquisitor also reminds Jesus, who offers humankind freedom, that 'the same crowds of common people who today kissed your feet will tomorrow at a single nod from me rush to rake up the coals at your stake'. In other words, you have to keep the bread and miracles coming or the populace will turn on you. Freedom alone is far too abstract a blessing, and miracles too haphazard, to satisfy the common folk for long.

———

For a multitude of reasons, by 1991 the bread supply for the mass of the population had become very shaky indeed, and, as far as miracles were concerned, in the clear light of day and a freer press most of those were turning out to be no more than sleight of hand. Who was to blame for the people's torment? Gorbachev, the man who foolishly believed he could deliver both bread and freedom. Right on cue, millions of people began to clamour for more bread. A choice of deodorants was a very fine thing, and a package tour to Egypt, if you could afford it, beat a week in a sanatorium on the Volga hands down, but bread – food, heating, decent pensions, a good education, medical care – was an even finer thing and they rose up to defend their right to it. Or at least a host of Grand Inquisitor look-alikes waiting in the wings did so in their name. They came galloping in from every direction, these jumped-up cardinals of the True Church, sword in hand, pennants flying, promising an iron fist and miracles of the economic variety.

Two years later, in 1993, at the Oktyabrskaya metro station, I saw with my own eyes the people rising up again, intent on burning at the stake those it blamed (with some justification) for its misery and also for the loss of its empire. The Grand Inquisitor foresaw the consequences of that particular catastrophe, the loss of empire, as well: 'the need for universal unity,' he told Jesus, who may have felt a tremor of fellow feeling at this point, 'is the third and last torment of men.' They would always strive to organise themselves into a 'world state'. Little wonder that in 1991 Zhirinovsky, the extreme nationalist, like a lunatic from *The Possessed*, ranted on about depositing nuclear waste along the borders of the Baltic republics and blowing the radiation across their territory with giant fans until the rebellious Balts all sickened and died. In mad diatribes calculated to cast a spell on the populace, he fantasised about solving the Muslim problem by driving Uzbek and Tadjik troops against the Afghans until the home-grown Muslims were all dead. To this day in Russia even liberals, lunching in chic restaurants on the Arbat, flipping through *Cosmopolitan* while they regale you with details of their weekend in Paris, bemoan the loss of the empire. 'Imagine!' they say, rolling their eyes. 'I have to go to Kiev next weekend to see my brother and *I have to get a visa!*' Not that their independence has done the Ukrainians an ounce of good, they hasten to tell you. The country is a shambles. And the Ukraine is paradise compared to Georgia, Armenia, Turkmenistan, Tadjikistan . . . mad dictators, starvation, Muslim extremists, civil war, ecological disaster, corruption, crime, gang warfare – except for the Muslim element, they make it sound like South America in the seventies.

AFTER A DAY OR TWO of walking Moscow's streets with a ghostly Dostoyevsky by my side, I was not as astonished by what I saw as I had been that first morning on the drive into the suburbs from the Leningrad Station. What I was looking at, I realised, was an eerie twilight zone between bread and freedom.

On the streets of central Moscow bread seemed to be in plentiful supply. What a pleasure it was after all these years, as it had been in St Petersburg, to be able to drop in to a clean, friendly café at the drop of a hat and order a *caffelatte* and a slice of strudel. It brought a smile to my lips (of course it did) to sit watching the crowds milling about in the Arbat like any crowd at home: there were dreadlocks, ponytails, crewcuts and expensive perms; kids in LA street chic, matrons in up-to-the-minute outfits and good shoes (old women had disappeared as if by magic) and men straight out of the pages of *GQ* (which was on sale, in fact, in the kiosk opposite); at street stalls they were flicking through racks of CDs and DVDs, they were text-messaging their friends, they were browsing for a new laptop computer; they were open-faced, good-humoured (for the most part), they were even walking the way we walk. (I remember in the sixties an Estonian friend telling me he could see me coming along the street from a long way off. 'It's the way you Westerners walk,' he said. 'We don't walk like that in the Soviet Union.') They knew that when they got home there would be toothpaste and toilet-paper in the bathroom, a selection of good things to eat in the refrigerator, and a bit of harmless nonsense to fall asleep over on the box later in the evening. They'd been globalised. They could think more or less whatever they pleased, too, despite the muzzled media, and even say quite a lot of it aloud, much as I could. This was all a joy. Not unbelievable, but a joy nonetheless.

Out in the suburbs where I was staying, deep in the endless forest of high-rise apartments, the crowds outside the metro station looked shiftier than those in the city centre, less sure that the refrigerator would be full or their children occupied with nothing more sinister in their bedrooms than computer games, but downtown the people clearly had bread. Indeed, if all the Audis, BMWs, Parisian fashion outlets, jewellery stores and elite apartment blocks for the new gentry were anything to go by, a lot of people had a lot of it. How their lips would curl, I thought, if they could see the lustreless provincial city I live in (which once they'd have given their eyeteeth to visit). Not a single elite apartment block, five-star hotel or Dolce & Gabbana boutique on the whole island. For that matter, no gentry.

Miracles in the Grand Inquisitor's sense of the word were also on offer again, it seemed. There were freshly painted domes and spires sprouting everywhere amongst the tower-blocks. Officially, at least, miracles appeared to be back in the hands of the Orthodox Church, although, just as the Grand Inquisitor had predicted, the seers, diviners and magicians – black or white, take your pick – were also flourishing. The herd will clamour, he said, 'for the miracle of the witch-doctor and the sorcery of the wise woman', and, if the advertisements in the press were any guide, from Odessa to the Bering Strait the herd was doing precisely that. Someone still has to dispense miracles, after all, and the present regime seems to have lost its taste for manipulating the smoke and mirrors, settling for authority instead. On high holidays, needless to say, 'the king, the court, the knights, the cardinals, and the fairest ladies of the court' (to quote Ivan Karamazov) – the new regime, in other words – attend services in the capital's magnificently restored temples, just as they did in Dostoyevsky's Seville. Do they believe? Probably not, but for the court that is never the point of the exercise.

———

What struck me, now I was back in Moscow poking about at my leisure, was not that nothing had changed, but that, despite a freer marketplace and more freedom of speech, the Grand Inquisitor still ruled. His view of humanity as base and weak, 'innately lawless', still held, while his belief in the need to wield the Sword of Caesar and his contempt for individual freedom seemed as strong as they had been in the time of Ivan the Terrible or Leonid Brezhnev. You need more than a few Burger Kings and a parliament to change the culture of the Grand Inquisitor. At least under Ivan the Terrible and Leonid Brezhnev the powerless hordes had believed in the existence of a kind of covenant between the rulers and the ruled – dimly, even mistakenly, but they had believed in it. Not any more.

Sinning is permitted in the new Russia, naturally, as it was in Dostoyevsky's Seville. The Soviet regime never quite understood the importance of allowing the masses to sin. 'Oh, we shall permit them to sin,' the Grand Inquisitor assures Jesus, 'they are weak and helpless, and they will love us like children for allowing them to sin. We shall tell them that every sin can be redeemed, if committed with our permission . . . and they will submit to us cheerfully and joyfully . . .'

By all accounts sexual debauchery in particular is almost *de rigueur* in post-Soviet Russia – not that you'd notice on a casual stroll around the city. Frankly, to my eyes eros seemed almost absent from Moscow's streets. In Australia, not to mention Paris or Berlin, every inch of public space has been so thoroughly eroticised that we barely notice the erotic any more. Every newspaper advertisement, every hoarding, shop window and magazine cover, every talk show and police drama on television, even the way people walk and dress and perform themselves in public in the West, is calculated to stimulate the erotic imagination, to coax to the surface our deeply ingrained narcissism. In Russia they have all the latest props now – the hoardings and window displays, the clothes and the haircuts, the soap-operas and talk shows – but few have learnt to play the game. At least, not in the street. APARTMENTS FOR SALE OR LEASE reads the billboard – but there's no picture of a sexy young couple about to go to bed in their new apartment. BOOKS, BEAUTY SALON, BED LINEN, CAFE, SUSHI BAR, SECOND-HAND CLOTHING, WINSTON, SONY . . . but where's the double entendre, the slinky blonde, the square-jawed urban cowboy, the risqué wording to egg us on? Where is the play on debauched self-indulgence? Why is nobody trying to seduce anyone? A strapping blonde pops up on hoardings here and there advertising German beer, but even she, by Western standards, looks oddly unerotic, as if she were promoting a cure for abdominal bloating.

The reason is simple: in Russia sex (it's called *seks*, of course) is still sin, not a way of life. It's 'raising hell', in Dostoyevsky's phrase, not part and parcel of your everyday self. Sin flowers lushly here now, after the overthrow of Soviet puritanism, but for the most part, it would seem, at night in special hothouses: gentlemen's clubs, casinos with raunchy late shows, erotic nightclubs, not to mention the foyer of my hotel in St Petersburg. At breakfast-time we had a chaste harpist plucking away while we ate our muesli, but in the foyer the night before the parade of slender, glossy-haired beauties bent on sinning had been quite dazzling. At one restaurant in Moscow, so I'm told, even the guests strip off and dance naked on the tables. And should you care to look a little more closely at the magazines on sale in the kiosks around the city, you'll soon find, tucked away amongst all the *Burdas* and *Cosmopolitans*, juicy little issues of 'health' magazines ('Try sex with one of these gadgets!' 'For answers to your sexual queries, turn to our Intimacy section!' 'How to seduce a normal man'), leisure magazines ('How to hide your lover's presents from your husband!' 'Bangkok's brothels: we let you in on their secrets!' 'Nudism and you'), as well as piles of less glossy magazines devoted to less glamorous kinds of sin (fetishistic excesses, for example, binge-drinking and enormities of a punkish kind). Selling you your copy of *The Egoist* (For Men Only), however, or *Speed* ('Her love affair with an Arab!') will almost certainly be a tired-looking, middle-aged woman with nothing more licentious on her mind than a night in front of the telly bickering with her half-sozzled husband over who should feed the cat.

Was I amazed by this post-Soviet explosion of sexuality? Not in the slightest. Hardly edified, of course, but not amazed. Apart from anything else, I'd seen it all before at home where, naturally enough, we also provide these services for those who still quaintly believe in sin. More to the point, I'd read 'The Grand Inquisitor'.

On the first weekend I managed to escape Moscow's high-rise sprawl by spending a few days staying with an old friend, Irina, at her house in the southern dacha belt beyond Moscow's outer ring road. On the Friday afternoon we hurtled southwards along the highway in a stream of fast-moving traffic heading for the countryside. Semi-trailers roared past us like maddened monsters. Sleek German limousines swished past one after the other like a never-ending volley of rockets. It was terrifying – worse than France.

I arrived at the dacha rattled and morose. The garden, which was just coming to life again after six months under snow, failed to charm me. Once inside the house, which was spacious and smelt deliciously of pinewood, all I felt was far from home. Every traveller succumbs from time to time to these moments of wanting to be somewhere else, but it can be hard on the locals. I knew I should have been making more of an effort.

We sat in the sun looking out at the garden and drank tea. In the old days it had been from Georgia, but this was Twining's. We'd known each other, Irina and I, since my first stint at Moscow University in the mid-sixties. In that time the world had turned upside down, but we seemed to have changed very little. Sitting across the table from me in the spring sunshine was precisely the same Irina I'd spent every spare moment with in Brezhnev's Moscow. Wars, ideologies, fashions, husbands, even one wife, had come and gone, but we were disconcertingly the same. In various incarnations in the ensuing years, we'd met up in Moscow, Leningrad, Tallinn and even Sydney once border controls had been loosened; we'd written hundreds of letters to each other, telephoned across continents, grown close, grown apart, then closer again. Even my funny Moscow accent is partly her fault. Yet, after forty years, while knowing each other inside out, we still don't quite understand each other. So she knew I was unhappy, but didn't really understand why. And I knew she knew but couldn't explain.

Irina was (and had always been) something I've never quite understood: she was 'loyal', *loyalna* – it's a foreign word, but a Russian concept. She'd read Solzhenitsyn (in the versions I had smuggled in), she knew about the concentration camps, she knew about the barbed wire encircling her country, she knew what fear was, she hadn't a Marxist bone in her body, she knew about life in the bourgeois West, she appreciated how free we were by comparison . . . but she was loyal. To what, exactly? I've never quite understood. To something, I suppose, which hardly exists in a country like Australia. Not to a leader, a regime, an ideology or a religion. To her *rodina*, perhaps, her native land, and its dense storyline, in which she has had her part to play and which has unfolded here, in these streets, houses, fields and forests and nowhere else. As a result there's a rootedness to her existence which I can only envy. She, for her part, has never quite understood my lack of loyalty to anything, my strangely haphazard trajectory. So, while we both know how to love, we come at love from different directions.

'You seem out of sorts,' she said. 'Why don't you have a rest?'

'No, I'm not tired.'

'What about a walk, then? We could take the dogs to the ponds and watch the fishermen fishing. Or the forest – we could go for a stroll in the forest.' There was a fringe of dark green on the hillside behind the dachas across the road.

'I'm happy to just sit here talking.' Just sitting talking is, after all, what people have always done at their dachas.

What I couldn't say was what I can never easily say to Europeans: why walk in your thin forest when it's littered with junk and surrounded by hundreds of houses all looking the same? Why walk across your tired fields to your ponds when there's an eight-lane highway and a railway-line just over the hill? Why go anywhere at all when from the Urals to the Irish Sea there's nothing but people, people, people and more people? So full – and yet also so strangely empty (to my antipodean eyes).

Irina's dacha, to be fair, actually stands on the edge of quite a pretty town – it's not situated in one of the new post-Soviet 'villages' called Sherwood (or something equally pretentious) surrounding the larger towns, nor does it sport fake castles or Californian bungalows. All the same, I felt as hemmed in by the urban blight in her dacha as I did in Moscow. We sat without saying anything for a moment, listening to the drone of a plane taking off from some nearby airport. I knew I was being ungracious.

'I can see why you love coming to the dacha on weekends,' I began as warmly as I could. 'The garden, the fruit-trees, the space – you can breathe here.' Irina and her husband live in a small apartment high up in a tower-block on the edge of Moscow's sprawl. You reach it in a lift covered in startling graffiti. ('Don't you dare read any of it!' she said as the doors closed. 'I forbid it.') Downstairs between the tower-blocks there's a courtyard with a few trees where people of all ages with nothing else to do sit watching their neighbours come and go. It isn't squalid or gloomy, as inner-city courtyards can be, but there is something about it, something about the people sitting and wandering about in it, which Dostoyevsky would have known how to capture with one stroke of his pitiless pen. Just beyond the block next door to Irina's is a highway hopelessly clogged with trucks and cars trying to get onto and off the ringroad. There's a well-stocked supermarket nearby, though, near the entrance to the underground. Not yet quite Paris or even Hobart, but almost, and utterly unimaginable out there in the Moscow suburbs just a few years ago.

Irina wasn't fooled by my remarks about the fruit-trees and breathing fresh air. 'You still don't much like Moscow, do you?' How she'd have loved me to say it had bowled me over.

'I don't like big cities any more.'

She smiled. 'I thought that this time you might like it more.'

'Why? Because of the new supermarkets and cappuccinos?'

Did I dislike Moscow? Could you like Moscow? Could anyone like an endless landscape of frigid white towers and super-highways.

Old Moscow, huddled, yellowing, squatting in tree-lined circles around the Kremlin, had its charms. Especially on Sundays when everyone was out walking and the streets were empty of cars. The English traveller John Foster Fraser had liked it very much in 1901. A 'blend of garish Tartar and drab European', he'd called 'wonderful Moscow', crowded in those days with Byzantine churches glowing gaudily in the ruddy haze of late afternoon. It wasn't Victorian London, but it wasn't Ulan Bator, either. Something in between. There are few 'Tartar' touches left nowadays – perhaps he meant the pre-Petrine grotesque, so outlandish to the English eye – but he'd still feel at home in these older parts of town, I'm sure. Still, none of this was the point and Irina knew it.

'Moscow's basically an imperial city,' I said at last. 'It was the centre of the Soviet empire. The Moscow I knew was built to crush you. And I still feel crushed by it. The supermarkets and cappuccinos don't change anything.' My mind flew home to Hobart, where the gardens, squares, streetscapes and houses are built to delight and amuse, and occasionally to impress (not always with finesse), but never to crush. Still, that wasn't the point, either, and she knew it.

'I really like being here,' I said, truthfully but treading carefully, 'and I'm . . . overjoyed – truly, I'm overjoyed – to see you living normally.' ('Normal' is an inoffensive word in Russian. 'How are things?' Russians ask when they meet. 'Normal,' they reply.) What I meant was: I'm delighted that you can go to Austria for your summer holidays, surf the internet, dress like a Charlottenburg matron and offer me mango juice, camembert on French bread and Finnish yogurt for lunch – borrow like us at last, in other words, join our comfortable world of mass-produced mediocrity. But I also wanted to say that at some important level, from my point of view, nothing had changed: mass-produced mediocrity was still mass-produced mediocrity, whether it came from Minsk or Kansas; Seville, as far as I could make out, was still pretty much Seville; there was still a Grand Inquisitor running the show; and Russian civilisation was still grounded in the view that the mass of human beings was base and weak, unworthy of any kind of freedom that mattered. The freedoms that mattered were the preserve of the 'hundred thousand who ruled over them', in Dostoyevsky's words, who, by the way, looked uncannily like the hundred thousand who had ruled over them a few decades earlier. Might this not be the reason, I'd have liked to suggest, that there'd been no reckoning in post-Soviet Russia, no penance and no punishment for the hundreds of thousands of gaolers, butchers and thieves or their millions of accomplices? There was no need for either penance or punishment because at root, unlike in Germany after the war, the old regime was still running the show.

I said none of these things. Irina knew her *Brothers Karamazov* as well as I did. We'd studied Dostoyevsky together at Moscow University. Besides, she was loyal.

'Don't tell me you're nostalgic for the old days,' she said, with a touch of annoyance. It's a common come-back when Russians sense that you are less than stunned by the changes. A successful businesswoman, she was doing well in the new Russia. Despite bankruptcy, robberies and all the upheaval, she was flourishing, and I was pleased about that. She really did go to Austria for her summer holidays. She found Helsinki a bore.

'No, I'm not nostalgic for anything,' I said, 'except being young, of course. Or if I *am* nostalgic, it's for something that might have been, not something that was.'

'Give us time.'

'Look,' I said, 'it's like a marriage. What I feel for Russia is like a husband's feelings for his wife after fifty years of marriage. Once it was an intoxicating love affair – even the disagreements were exciting. Now it's – well, it's a marriage. It's almost your whole life, it's what you are, but, at the same time, it's driving you beserk.'

'I seem to recall,' she said with a smile, 'that you don't much believe in marriage.'

Touché! Feeling much better to have got all that off my chest, I took up her suggestion to take the dogs for a walk over to the fishing ponds. The dogs went mad with joy.

DURING THOSE FIRST FEW DAYS in Moscow my efforts to unearth traces of Turgenev were half-hearted at best. Although it was the city he'd spent some years in as a boy, going to school there and then at the age of fifteen enrolling for a year at Moscow University (which was 'full of nitwits', in his opinion), it was never really his city. He came and went all his life – he could hardly get to France from his estate at Spasskoye without doing so – but, even as I walked past his old school in Gagarinsky Pereulok (emblazoned with a hammer and sickle and the words UP WITH THE USSR) or the old university buildings where he'd once rubbed shoulders with Herzen and other intellectual luminaries (without having the faintest idea who they were), I knew in my bones that I would hear no echoes of Turgenev's voice.

Around the corner from his school, on Gogolevsky Boulevard, I even ducked into the small palace belonging to a friend of his where he once kept a flat, waking every morning to the bells of the small red church nearby. It's occupied by an artists' union these days and has a shop and a bar on the ground floor just inside the grand colonnaded entrance. I walked up the staircase and peered about, but felt nothing. Turgenev's presence here, despite the off-hand plaque by the front door ('On a number of occasions the great Russian writer Ivan Sergeyevich Turgenev stayed in this house'), had become just a tale that was told.

In St Petersburg a week earlier, fresh off the plane from Paris, I'd felt more hopeful of being propelled back, even momentarily, into his world, to see what he saw and to catch some faint echo of his voice – or at least of the voices in his books. The houses, the streets, the churches and the canals were still largely there, but the voices were very muffled.

St Petersburg simply doesn't recognise Turgenev as one of its writers, although he was a student there as well, lived there at various times and visited on and off all his life. On dingy Podyacheskaya Street, for example, is the house where he was living when he first heard Viardot sing. It's unmarked.

The vast golden dome of St Isaac's Cathedral rearing up above the houses at the end of the street is an awe-inspiring sight these days, although, when he was falling in love, setting off for the theatre or the Viardots' apartment, he would scarcely have noticed it – it wasn't quite finished in 1843. Standing across the road from his house, just looking at it, I felt no quickening of my imagination. I wanted to fly back across the gap between then and now, but it was unbridgeable.

Around Nevsky Prospekt – somewhat spruced up since my last visit, but with the same yellowish, dignified dowdiness about it that it had always had; it will never be the Champs Elysées – the resonances were scarcely any louder, drowned out by the din of modernity. On one corner, for instance, stands the Grand Hotel where in the spring of 1879, already a famous writer, Ivan Sergeyevich found himself seriously smitten with the young actress Maria Savina.

No echoes there, not even a murmur.

I toyed with the idea of having a coffee in the outdoor café, just to feel I'd been there, but it would probably have cost an arm and a leg, so I wandered off to the Republic of Coffee instead and sat in a daze in its smoky darkness, listening to funky American music. Everyone was wearing black, just as they do at home in such places. The notices on the walls were in English. I could hardly believe I was in Russia. At last after all these years I was back on Nevsky Prospekt, somewhere I should belong, yet I found I didn't belong there at all. Not any more. I downed my coffee and fled.

––––

Further along the Nevsky, on the corner of the Fontanka canal, is the house Ivan Sergeyevich's friend and mentor, the critic Vissarion Belinsky, lived in for four years. Gazing up at the windows of the flat, though, I couldn't catch even a whisper of the frenzied, late-night conversations Turgenev must have taken part in as a young man here. I have always felt a great fondness for Belinsky. He's famous for once shouting out in the small hours of the morning, while spitting up blood (perhaps in this very flat): 'Home? You can't go home – we haven't yet decided whether or not God exists!' He is even more famous for his 'Letter to Gogol', an outraged attack on a writer he loved passionately but for the wrong reasons, written, as it happens, in 1847 in Germany while he was travelling through Europe with Turgenev. What Gogol had failed to realise, he thundered – wounding

Gogol terribly – was that 'Russia sees her salvation not in mysticism, asceticism or pietism, but in the progress of civilisation, enlightenment and humane values. What she needs,' he went on, always knowing best, 'are not sermons (she has heard enough of them) or prayers (she has repeated them enough) but the awakening in the people of a sense of human dignity', which had been trampled for centuries in the mud and dirt.

Needless to say, Belinsky was proposing a completely different view of civilisation from the tsar's, who made it a crime even to read his letter. It was a view that was close to Turgenev's heart, however, all his life, although I dare say he'd have expressed himself to Gogol with more generosity of spirit than Belinsky, at least in writing.

Just across the canal, at Fontanka No. 38, is the house where Turgenev worked on his first novel, *Rudin*, and sketched out the ideas for his second, *Nest of the Gentry*. There's an Italian boutique in the building now, with a bed-and-breakfast establishment and an English bookshop next door. It was here that Tolstoy came to stay with him in 1855, fresh from the Crimean front. The plaque by the door reads:

In this house
from 19 November 1855 to 1 January 1856
lived the great Russian writer
Lev Nikolayevich Tolstoy

Not a syllable about his host. I took umbrage and stalked off. ('You must be mistaken,' a tour guide said to me later when I commented on the omission. I thought he'd be sympathetic and interested, but he stood firmly on the side of the plaque-makers. A plaque was official. Turgenev had evaporated.)

Over the next couple of days I saw the house where he'd finished writing *Nest of the Gentry* and then listened to his friend Annenkov reading it back to him (he'd come down with laryngitis); I saw the house where years later he'd finished writing *Smoke* and then read it aloud to Annenkov. But I didn't catch a sound.

Over in the down-at-heel Dostoyevsky district ('That's where Raskolnikov killed the old woman with an axe!' the guide had bellowed into her loudspeaker as we glided past in our ferry) I eventually found a park named after Turgenev. There was a monument there to the Holy Mother of God, Queen of Heaven and Earth and of the City and our Country, but no monument to Turgenev. Across the road from the park I spotted the On the Eve gift shop, named after his third novel, but felt no desire to go in and browse. Over near the conservatorium (built on the site of the old Bolshoi Kamenny Theatre where Viardot had sung and, sitting on the gilded bear's paw, he'd fallen in love forever) – in fact, backing onto the very garden in which Rasputin was shot and bound in iron chains before being dumped into the canal – I chanced upon a restaurant named after his *Nest of the Gentry*.

Silence. Not even a sigh. Not even from Rasputin.

In all the time I was in St Petersburg, the only moment of recognition came when I was passing the Mariinsky Theatre one morning, a stone's throw from where Viardot had first sung in the Bolshoi, and suddenly, from across the canal, I heard a soprano practising her scales.

Perhaps I simply wasn't sure what I should be listening for. Or perhaps I found the new St Petersburg so bamboozling, so surreal – why was Leningrad pretending to be Helsinki? it just ended up looking blowsy – that I lacked the patience to wait for the voices I wanted to hear to rise above the roar and clatter?

I have an admission to make at this point: something about this Venice of the North, this Petrine fantasy of incomparable beauty, leaves me cold. I know it's a marvel, or at least looms up out of its swamps like the vision of a marvel, I know it 'affords dazzling prospects', as the brochure in my hotel room assured me, I know every brick, every stone in the city has an amazing story to tell, but it leaves me largely unmoved. It's not Venice at all, of course, or even Rome. It's a grandiose imperial fantasy strung out along a river in the middle of nowhere. Let me hide behind John Foster Fraser, who wrote in *The Real Siberia* in 1901: 'St Petersburg is too modern, too cosmopolitan to please eyes fond of the picturesque. The buildings are usually imitations of something else, and the marble, not infrequently, is painted plaster. There is a T-square arrangement of thoroughfares which is useful, but not pretty. There are palaces to be seen. But palaces are the same the world over – the same endless galleries, with the same giant vases, gilt bedsteads and slippery floors . . . Moscow is far better.'

Few, I suppose, apart from Muscovites, would agree with him these days, but a century ago, for a traveller looking for the 'real Russia', I dare say he had a point.

NOTHING ON THE JOURNEY from Moscow to Spasskoye was as I'd imagined it would be. Not a thing. Not the squalid villages, clinging like scabs to the slopes beside the road south from the capital; nor the lushly undulating countryside around Mtsensk, all green and black and watery beneath a soft lilac sky (I think I'd pictured plains criss-crossed by ravines, Courtavenel with birch groves). And I certainly hadn't expected the small brick café emblazoned with Coca-Cola signs in the Spasskoye carpark. What would the Great Russian Writer have made of *that*, I wondered? (The café was open, but not serving either tea or coffee. 'This isn't a *shop*, you know,' the waitress snapped over her shoulder and then went back to washing curtains in a bucket. I felt immediately at home.)

The house itself was nothing like the Spasskoye of my imagination, either. I knew that the old manor house of Turgenev's childhood was no longer to be seen in its entirety, most of it having burnt down while Turgenev was away in Berlin as a young student. Although the guidebooks (and the guides themselves, as it turned out) were fuzzy on the details, it was clear that there would be little left to see of *that* Spasskoye, seat of his mother's feudal domains, poised like an owl, as they used to say, with its two curved wings stretched out behind it, about to swoop on prey it had spotted amongst the oaks and limes in the surrounding park. That Spasskoye, with its offices, theatre, hospital, police station and stables, all swarming with serfs dressed up as butlers, ladies-in-waiting, lackeys, maids, cooks, singers, musicians, clerks, bailiffs and gardeners, would obviously have to stay a picture in my head.

All the same, I'd expected something grander than the house I caught sight of amongst the trees not far from the main gates: a modest, two-storeyed, wooden affair with two verandas (upstairs and down) and faded mauve paintwork, hardly bigger than a large dacha. No one had promised me Blenheim Palace, Turgenev's mother had not been in the Sheremetyev or Stroganov class, but I hadn't been prepared for a weatherboard weekender, either, the sort of thing any suburban bank manager at home might build for himself with a bit of help from his brother.

Making my way towards it past the church covered in scaffolding just inside the gates, I found it hard to picture Turgenev's mother, Varvara Petrovna, ringing bells in this house to summon her Postmaster, Chamberlain and Ministers (all serfs, of course) as she was wont to do, like the ruler of some down-at-heel minor principality on the Rhine. Yet this was the house she left him when she died, the house he sought refuge in when his first love for Pauline Viardot petered out, the house he then wrote his true masterpieces in (all in a rush, spurred on by love gone wrong) and the house he constantly came back to from Baden-Baden and Paris during his second love for Viardot, right up until two years before he died. It just wasn't at all the sort of house in which, in my mind's eye, I'd had Turgenev (and quite a few of his characters) wandering about, drinking tea, writing letters, arguing, falling in love, singing duets, spending sleepless nights and listening to the chaffinches chirping in the garden.

Inside the house things weren't quite right, either: the rooms were all so small, so spotless, the exquisite furniture so sparse and highly polished. I'd imagined something more spacious, higher-ceilinged, the rooms furnished for living on a grander scale.

Our little group stood in silent reverence in its one-size-fits-all felt slippers – all Russian museums insist on this Donald Duck footwear – now in the dining-room, now the parlour, the living-room . . . it was all so intimate, so ordinary. I half expected to see Ivan Sergeyevich come padding through in his dressing-gown and slippers, murmuring 'Do excuse me!' on his way to the bathroom. (We were actually never shown the bathroom – one never is – although we would every last one of us have given our eye-teeth to see it.)

To be frank, even more disconcerting than the smallness of everything was the suspicion that even this remaining wing of the old manor was almost entirely a recent reconstruction. Why did it matter? I'm not sure why – it's not as if I thought Turgenev's ghost had gone up in smoke along with the house, I hadn't even expected a ghost. Apparently, in 1906 the then empty house had burnt to the ground and was only rebuilt (or, in some versions, restored) seventy years later. After nearly a century of fires and pillaging, not to mention the German occupation, it was filled once more with Turgenev's own furniture, paintings, books and belongings. So what we now saw, as we dutifully inspected his dining-table, his china, his bed and the divan he used to stretch out on just inside the front door awaiting guests, was apparently more or less what Turgenev had seen on his last visit to

Spasskoye, not long before he died. We could put ourselves in his shoes. We could re-enact being Turgenev. But it wasn't – and I apologise for resorting to such an old-fashioned expression – quite the real thing. This Spasskoye, in other words, was theatre, a tableau we could take part in, rather than a sacred site.

It was markedly more sacred, however, than the Turgenev museum in Oryol, the town an hour's drive away where my driver Kolya and I had spent the previous night.

This museum, whose every room is filled to overflowing with memorabilia, is in a large old house Turgenev never set foot in. As Kolya and I wandered from room to room, past lithographs, paintings, his mother's blouse, his student notes from Berlin, manuscripts, letters, first editions, books from his library, furniture from Spasskoye, portraits of uncles and fellow writers he once met, his brother's birth certificate, pictures of Baden-Baden, Naples and La Scala (which he visited), his desk from the rue de Douai, posters of films based on his works . . . as we passed from room to room in dazed silence past all these objects connected with Turgenev's life, a morose attendant trailed behind us, turning out the lights. Kolya was very taken with it all. In fact, until that afternoon in the museum, despite a basic Soviet education in a small town down near the Ukrainian border, he hadn't had the faintest idea who Turgenev was, apart, of course, from recognising the name as belonging to a Great Russian Writer.

'So . . . Turgenev owned serfs, did he?' Kolya asked, when we found ourselves back out on the street.

'Well, yes, he did,' I said, 'thousands of them – or at least his mother did, and he inherited them.'

We ambled off towards the centre of Oryol, a few quiet streets away. 'Didn't you read "Mumu" at school?' I asked. Surely he'd read 'Mumu', the still heart-breaking story based on Varvara Petrovna's brutal treatment of a serf. (The barking of a serf's dog, the only creature in the world he loves, disturbs her, so she forces him to drown it.) All Soviet schoolchildren read 'Mumu'.

'"Mumu" . . . yes,' he said, 'we did. But I didn't know it was about *him*.'

'Drowning dogs wasn't the half of it,' I said. By this time we were crossing Lenin Square, dodging roller-skaters and parties of schoolchildren being dragged off to see something that would be good for them. 'His mother regularly had her peasants flogged – for not weeding the flower-beds properly, for example, or for dropping a cup – she regularly flogged Ivan, for that matter, just to keep him on his toes. She sold her peasants off like cattle – worse: like old furniture – when it suited her, breaking up families and taking children away from their parents, although she always prided herself on the way she kept her serfs better fed and better clothed than most of her neighbours did. She even taught some of her favourites to read.'

Kolya didn't seem much moved. The iniquities of the tsarist regime were old news.

'All the same,' I went on, determined nonetheless that he should have a vivid picture of just what a wicked woman Turgenev's mother had been, 'everyone on her estate lived in fear. She was capable of sending a man off to certain death in the army for failing to bow low enough as he passed her window. She was vicious and mad. Mind you, she came from a whole line of barbarians. She was appallingly mistreated as a child. Her mother hated her, her step-father beat her and tried to rape her . . . and her husband slept with half the province.'

Kolya still didn't seem much moved. Brutality and living in fear were no novelty to Kolya. In fact, we were passing Lenin's statue while I was holding forth.

'Ilyich,' Kolya said, in case I hadn't realised who the bronze figure towering above us was.

'So I see.'

'To look at this square, you'd think we were back in the old Soviet Union,' he said, with a quick chortle.

'Not quite, surely.' True, it was a vast, empty square named after Lenin in the middle of town, surrounded on all sides by bland Soviet-era buildings (the provincial government buildings, a couple of hotels, the Turgenev Theatre) as well as one or two reminders of nineteenth-century Oryol, which had been a prosperous, highly gentrified city, with numerous fine town houses and impressive churches. And yes, it had that slightly eerie Soviet quiet about it. It was certainly hard to believe that we were standing in the throbbing heart of a city of nearly half a million people. There's more happening in downtown Hobart, a city less than half the size of Oryol, at midnight on a Tuesday than on Oryol's main square at peak hour.

At the same time, something about the square was not Soviet at all. It wasn't just the roller-skaters, either, in their Adidas tops, gabbling into their mobile phones at Lenin's feet or the woman with the Marks & Spencer carrier bag getting out of her Audi. No, it was something less obvious than these fairly superficial signs of a globalised economy. 'What is it, then?' Kolya was curious.

'I think it's the absence of fear,' I said – and then regretted it. It was true, but, putting it like that, I felt I'd struck the wrong note. What I'd meant to say was that I sensed a movement outwards on the streets of Oryol, rather than a closing-in, as I once would have felt in a town like this, an inclination to flirt with life rather than retreat from it. And that was new. Perhaps it was more a matter of a newly awakened greed than curiosity – it was hard to tell. Kolya didn't comment.

———

Just opposite Lenin, on the corner of Lenin Square and Lenin Street, stood our hotel, the Rus (the ancient name for Russia – it rhymes with 'goose'). The *Lonely Planet* had made it clear that we should not expect too much of the Rus (apart from 'night calls concerning intimate services'), but it had turned out to be remarkably comfortable, its staircase decorated with the portraits of famous writers from the region and a friendly little buffet on the second floor open around the clock.

In fact, although I'd been warned by Muscovite friends (who these days tend to know Paris better than the provinces) not to expect too much of Oryol in general, it struck me on that first afternoon as quite a pleasant, clean and relatively affluent place. My *Lonely Planet* guide remarks on its 'rosy simplicity', and I could see what it meant: there's a pleasing dignity about the pastel-coloured buildings lining its streets, at least in the centre of town.

In Moscow, as I had been preparing to set off, they'd muttered more darkly still about the dearth of anywhere decent to eat, or even to drink a decent cup of coffee, on the five-hour drive south. As it turned out, there had been a roadside café offering a remarkable array of things to eat and drink every few miles from the Moscow ringroad all the way to Oryol. I was reminded, when we stopped in the middle of nowhere at one smart little establishment with a twelve-page menu, of a passage in John Foster Fraser's account of his trip across Siberia by train in 1901: he was staggered by the refreshment-rooms he found at wayside stations 'with not a house within sight; with, indeed, nothing but heaving dreary prairie around': not only were the waiters in the Siberian wilderness 'dressed as are waiters in Piccadilly hotels', but on long tables covered with clean cloths there would be rye bread, wine, 'hot dishes, half fowls, beef steaks, meat pies, basins of soup'. Russians like their refreshments, and always have done, even if the Soviet economy made indulging their appetite rather dicey.

We sat, Kolya and I, in the buffet of the Hotel Rus for a while that first evening, snacking more modestly on fish sandwiches, Mars Bars and Nescafé, our eyes glued to a particularly brutal Russian version of *The Weakest Link*. When the news from the panic-stricken world outside began, an avalanche as usual of bombings and mass slaughter, Kolya suggested a stroll in the Park of Culture and Rest on the high side of the river across the road. I love a good *passeggiata* in the early evening, and promenading is something Russians have a flair for. We don't do it where I come from. There's a flurry of jogging and dog-walking along the beach-front near my house at the end of the day, and a bit of milling about at the Saturday market, but no real *passeggiata*. If we want to socialise or show off, we invite people around for dinner.

This is my Russia, I thought to myself as we entered the park – it's still here! I melted with pleasure. Yes, the park was dotted with garish Coca-Cola signs and new cafés, and the strolling crowds were smartly dressed – not quite Baden-Baden perhaps, although they could easily have been Parisians (depending on the *arrondissement*, naturally) – but otherwise it could have been any Park of Culture and Rest from my youth: old men playing chess in the dappled sunshine; young men under the trees playing trashy love-songs on their guitars; packs of shaven-headed boys, like gangs of brutal angels, prowling around the dilapidated shooting-gallery and the billiards shed; girls striding along the avenues arm in arm, pretending they were on their way some-where; teenagers perched like seagulls on the backs of the benches, chattering; ice-cream vendors; lovers; and, of course, surrounded by a blaze of red tulips, a statue in honour of a Great Russian Writer (Turgenev). In fact, according to a notice on the main avenue through the park, Turgenev himself once 'strolled' here, as did Tolstoy and another noted local writer, Leskov (the Shostakovich opera *Lady Macbeth of the Mtsensk District* is based on one of his short stories). People have been strolling in this park for 180 years.

Hardly a soul there was alone, I noticed, just the odd office-worker cutting across the park to the bus stop. The park was an event rather than a place, an activity you took part in, not somewhere to sit and think. It was a game, an entertainment, a ritual, an opportunity to court life – if you had the wit. Over on the paved terrace near the gates groups of girls and boys were standing about smoking, flaunting their youth and restlessly killing time.

'They look so bored,' I said to Kolya idly.

'They're waiting for their fate,' he said, without an ounce of pity.

———

We headed back to the hotel. Under the watchful eye of the *dezhurnaya* – the duty floor-manager or Woman on the Floor, as we used to call her, a hangover from Soviet times; God alone knows what these alarming women do all day in the post-Soviet era – I went back to my room to stare out of the window and Kolya went back to his to watch some football-match live from Barcelona. Whether he was also offered services of a more intimate kind as the evening wore on, he did not divulge. My only adventure that night was being caught in the shower when the water was cut off.

So at Spasskoye next morning in that modest wooden house, by the time our group, faces frozen in reverence, got to Turgenev's tiny claret-coloured study, I was feeling all askew inside. After all, for me this spot was the living heart of Spasskoye. Here I was, after all these years and all those words (his, mine and hundreds of other people's), standing in his study beside his handsome desk with its green baize top, staring at his pen, the very pen I could imagine him penning *Nest of the Gentry* and *Fathers and Sons* with.

On the one hand, I felt as if I'd just collided with myself, met up with myself at last, as it were, after some thirty years. To put it another way, I felt that, by an extraordinarily circuitous route, I'd at last reached the very point in the universe where a second self had been standing timelessly all along. It was the point where on mornings exactly like this one – and on snowy afternoons and late at night by the light of the candle still standing on his desk – Ivan Sergeyevich Turgenev had written the words I had once threaded into my own soul. (He had never *pierced* me the way some writers can, I must admit, he'd never hurled me into some new dimension, but over the years I'd woven whole skeins of him into who I was.) So it was a little like coming home.

On the other hand, standing there on the (apparently) new parquet in my huge felt slippers, numbed by the high-pitched chirruping of the guide ('*V tysyacha vosemsot pyatdesyat shestom godu Ivan Sergeyevich . . . a v aprele tysyacha vosemsot pyatdesyat sedmogo goda Ivan Sergeyevich . . .*'), I also couldn't help feeling I'd come to the wrong address. Or to the right address to find nobody home. It was deeply unsettling. I'd expected a moment of luminous resolution, but instead I just felt disoriented, out of kilter.

As soon as I could, without ruffling too many feathers, I whispered a few words to the spell-bound Kolya and slithered and slid in my out-size slippers back towards the exit. Outside, I thought, amongst the birches, limes and maples of what they called 'the park', I might be able (for want of a better expression) to get a truer measure of the man. In the strange green-black twilight the forest paths all vanished into, I might be able to get a surer grasp on just who or what it was I thought I was 'coming home' to. At that early hour it would be just the rooks and me. As soon as the school groups started to arrive it would be mayhem.

———

Turgenev, too, had come home to Spasskoye to 'catch up with himself', I reflected, sauntering off into the park and drinking in the quiet. (Just a few birdcalls. What would Ivan Sergeyevich have heard on a May morning like this? Hammering and sawing, probably, horses neighing, someone shouting in the distance, a burst of laughter, muf-fled gun-shots. He would have smelt mud and lilac.) He hadn't come home just to the mauve-painted house, of course, but to the fields, forests, villages and ponds surrounding it – the living landscape. What he loved to conjure up in his mind when he was away in France or Germany, he said, was the 'sound of nightingales, the smell of straw and of birch-tree buds, the sun and the puddles in the roads'. I suppose we all remember with heightened emotion the settings we became who we are in. Year after year he came home from Baden-Baden and Paris to look with new eyes at everything he'd known and then write about what he saw, being who he'd now become. (Why else come home?)

Once his mother had died (to the strains of a peasant orchestra she'd commanded to play polkas in the next room) and Spasskoye was his, it was his only nest – an empty one, in some conventional sense, but his. He had just got back from Courtavenel; Baden-Baden and Paris were still well in the future, unforeseeable. He filled his nest with his characters by the dozen. It was here, in a burst of creative energy in his late thirties – his first love for Pauline Viardot having been crushed and his second not yet born – that he began writing his novels, including *Nest of the Gentry* and *Fathers and Sons*, both, as it happens, about men coming home from big cities to the house where they'd grown up.

In fact, Lavretsky in *Nest of the Gentry* comes home (also from a love that fell apart in France) to an ancestral nest very like Spasskoye. He drives through 'lushly naked' countryside of exactly the kind Kolya and I had driven through that morning, past the same 'long, low hills', the same 'grey little villages' and ravines dotted with clumps of oak trees that we had just seen. Lavretsky comes back to silence, as if to the bottom of a river. 'I've spent the best years of my life loving a woman,' he reflects, gazing out the window at the garden where nothing, hardly even a bumblebee or gnat, is stirring. 'Perhaps it's the very dullness of this place that will bring me to my senses, calm me down and give me the strength to do, without feeling rushed, the things I have to do.'

And he listens to the quiet, as I did that morning, 'expecting nothing – yet at the same time as if in a state of constant expectation'.

———

Turgenev wrote those lines at Spasskoye in 1858, when Pauline Viardot's attachment to him was at its weakest (they'd seen each other only once or twice, fleetingly, in eight years) and his young man's passion for her was slowly turning into something else, not yet tested. I could just see him sitting on the verandah in front of me drinking tea, as he liked to do, listening to the bees humming and the rooks cawing, contemplating Lavretsky's fate.

In the event he was hard on Lavretsky.

Mistakenly thinking he is now a widower (just as Turgenev no doubt suspected that the object of his obsessive love was forever beyond reach), Lavretsky allows his feelings for a pious and virginal young woman called Liza to become 'love'. That is to say, he feels once again what he felt when he fell in love with his wife: 'his whole soul melted into a single feeling, a single desire, the desire for happiness, for possession, for love, for a woman's sweet love'.

Virgins often left men of Lavretsky's (and Turgenev's) generation moonstruck for a time. They seemed to promise heaven. In the sober light of day, however, Turgenev, like his acquaintance Brahms, was much more strongly attracted to married women. Brahms, thinking of his beloved Clara Schumann, explained it pithily: virgins only promise heaven, he said, while Clara shows it revealed to us.

Unsurprisingly, it all ends badly for Lavretsky. Not only does his tramp of a wife reappear on the scene, scotching any hope that he and Liza might 'melt' together into a single being, but she then ups and disappears again back to Paris, leaving him high and dry for good.

In point of fact, the prospects for Lavretsky and Liza were never the best, Liza having in a sense already been ravished by God, just as Pauline had been by music. At an early age 'the image . . . of God squeezed with a kind of sweet force into her soul,' Turgenev tells us with unusual directness, 'filling her with awe and reverence . . . and Christ became something close and familiar to her, almost kindred.' After an episode like this, any 'possession' Lavretsky had planned had little chance of fulfilment. In any case, souls that melt into a single feeling always come to a sticky end in Turgenev's stories. Although he pined for that single feeling – who doesn't? we've all read the books and seen the movies – at root he had no faith in it. It always unravelled over time into separate strands.

Nest of the Gentry is not his best-known novel, having caused nothing like the furore *Fathers and Sons* did three years later, but it's always struck me as the most quintessentially Turgenevan novel of the six. Certainly it was the most universally admired of them. Despite a few typically clunky scene-changes, his 'ear for emotion' (in Virginia Woolf's phrase) in this novel is at its most finely tuned, to my mind, his observations at their most effortlessly poetic – and in that sense I tend to think of it as 'the best' of his novels. Perhaps the best writing is always a kind of 'coming home to silence' and the breaking of it. Perhaps clear-eyed homecoming is what good writing is.

Down by the pond at the far edge of the wood (Turgenev's 'garden') I spotted a bench where I could sit for a while and percolate. Eventually the hordes would catch up with me even here – I could hear a few faint shouts in the distance already – but for the moment I had the pond, looking moody under the cloudy sky, all to myself.

It wasn't really what I'd have called a 'pond' (in my crude Australian fashion I'd have called it a 'dam'), but 'pond' is how the Russian word for it is always translated and it's certainly more picturesque. It's in a pretty gully, fringed with birches and limetrees, and across the dam wall a stone's throw from where I was sitting the old post road from Moscow to the Crimea used to pass. In fact, Catherine the Great is supposed to have trundled across this very dam wall in her carriage with Potemkin on the way back from her triumphal 'Tauride tour' in 1787 – together with the two hundred gilded coaches and who knows how many other carriages and drays in her entourage. It must have been quite a sight. I wondered if one of Turgenev's ancestors had offered the weary Empress refreshments. She was so exhausted by this time that she failed to attend the ball in her honour in nearby Tula. I couldn't for the life of me even begin to picture the scene.

What I could picture much more readily was the scene in *Nest of the Gentry* where Lavretsky, Liza, her mother and one or two others spend the late afternoon by the pond 'at the bottom of the garden', not far from the dam wall, idly fishing for carp and loach. The lilac is in bloom, as it was the morning I was there, the fish are flashing gold and silver in the sun, the reddish reeds are softly rustling in the breeze, and Lavretsky, already seriously smitten, sitting on the trunk of an over-hanging willow, starts making overtures to Liza, who is pretending to be fishing. It's 1842, and in the 1840s a respectable older gentleman (he's thirty-five, 'a man whose life is over') has to circle his tender young quarry with great care.

After a spot of harmless gossip of the kind we still indulge in when on the prowl ('Do you like So-and-so?' 'No.' 'Why not?'), they move on to religion, as Russians are still apt to do without the slightest embarrassment. It's the sort of conversation which Turgenev, a 'pitiful, old-fashioned Voltairean' like Lavretsky, no doubt often had with the Countess Lambert, the deeply pious St Petersburg lady he drew close to back in Russia during his estrangement from Pauline Viardot.

After he's held forth for a while 'about religion, its significance in human history and the significance of Christianity' (in which he does not believe, although he claims to have 'a deep respect for all convictions' – why, I can't imagine), Liza startles him by saying: 'The reason one must be a Christian is not in order to understand what heaven is . . . or the things of this world,' – that being what science is for, presumably – 'but because everyone must die.'

Lavretsky is startled. 'Why this talk of death?' he asks.

'I don't know. I think about it a lot.'

'A lot?'

'Yes.'

As did Turgenev, of course. As indeed most of us do, especially when we're very young and first realise we're standing in line to be slaughtered and then again when we're approaching the head of the queue.

Turgenev, however, had his eyes fixed on the unpleasantness ahead even during his middle years, a time when most of us manage to ignore the fact that we're in a queue at all. In our middle years we generally prefer to busy ourselves with building a nest, working our way up at the office and enjoying the view to the side. At just forty, however, the year after he finished *Nest of the Gentry*, Turgenev was already writing to a friend: 'Life hurries us and pushes us along like cattle . . . while death, the nimble butcher, lies in wait – and slaughters.' Although the thought of eternal extinction was no more comforting to Turgenev than it is to anybody else, it was this daily shuffling forwards towards the butcher, I think, that gave rise to his spiritual panic, rather than any contemplation of his eventual nothingness. What horrified him was the fact that this edging forwards was simply in the order of things, part of nature, with no one to appeal to against it. 'The naturalness of death is far more frightening than its suddenness or unusual form,' he wrote to Countess Lambert, for whom, like Liza, the solution was simple: religious faith. Turgenev was not about to argue with her ('Only religion can conquer this fear,' he agreed), but 'religion itself must become a natural need in a man,' he wrote, and in him it wasn't. If a man doesn't have a natural religious bent, he went on ruefully, 'all he can do is avert his eyes frivolously or stoically (and in essence it doesn't matter which).'

For Sanin, in *Torrents of Spring*, we might remember, even averting his eyes proves a patchy solution.

A handsome, wealthy man of fifty-two, living alone, he comes home from an evening of sparkling conversation with pleasant companions – the women attractive, the men talented and interesting – and is instantly overwhelmed by a sense of burning disgust with his life. 'He brooded on the vanity, the pointlessness, the vulgar falsity of all things human,' Turgenev writes of Sanin, now sprawled in his armchair at home in front the fire. 'Everywhere he saw the same endless futility . . . the same partly well-meaning, partly deliberate self-delusion . . . And then all of a sudden, when you least expect it, old age is upon you and with it the ever-growing fear of death, which gnaws away and undermines *everything*.' (That's interesting: why 'everything'?)

No matter what we do, in other words, to distract ourselves from where we are – the art, the love affairs, the drugs, the frantic experiments with magic and religion, the shuffling of positions in the queue – we're in an abattoir and one day it will be our turn to face the 'nimble butcher'. Sanin does not turn to religion to make sense of human life, but instead, as we know, he remembers his short-lived love for the Italian pastry-cook's daughter, Gemma, thirty years before.

At first this might seem like a fatuous response to the anguish overwhelming him. In the face of total extinction what possible comfort could there be in calling to mind a youthful infatuation? I'm sure that's more or less what I thought myself when I first read *Torrents of Spring*. By that time I was no longer 'very young' myself. In my late twenties, newly married, I'd just stepped across the threshold of those 'middle years' when most of us focus on a career, a mortgage and a family, crafting a life that (if you don't look too far ahead) seems to go somewhere and make sense. I understood about the queue, naturally, having seen death at close quarters, but had no sense of standing in it myself.

In 1970 I went back to Moscow to read everything I could about Turgenev. Six days a week, week after week, I would sit at my green desk in the Lenin Library, just across from the Kremlin, poring over a century's books and journals, tracking down every last review, comment and reminiscence I could order from the closely guarded stacks. I might have done better, I now think, to have read less and lived a little more.

Rereading now what I wrote about Turgenev when I got home, I think I understood quite well his anguish at finding faith impossible – what Russians call '*vera*', the conviction that something is true and can be acted upon (social theories, for example, the existence of God or, conversely, the allness of the material universe). I did not find conviction impossible, but I could see why he did and why he'd have felt a kind of terror. However, on rereading what I wrote, I think that in my youthfulness I did fail to take his anguish seriously.

In part his expressions of anguish struck me as rather self-indulgent. They smacked of Romantic posing. After all, even if gouty, he was rich, famous, talented, free and in many ways loved – so why this endless moaning and groaning about decay and death and the pointlessness of everything? *Everything?* Why his 'cold disgust' with life? Why all this carry-on about falling helplessly beneath the Juggernaut and 'the soundless depths of *Nichtsein*?' (And why write 'non-being' in German?)

In part, too, I was irritated by his dismissal of God. To be fair, what he dismissed was the existence of *Bog*. (Actually pronounced 'bawkh', this is the word Russians use for the Christian 'God'. It was meticulously spelt with a small 'b' throughout the Soviet period, as if this might somehow call the deity's bluff. 'Aphrodite' and 'Cinderella', of course, kept their capitals.). This *Bog* was something I actually had no time for myself. In the late twentieth century, I would have said, who could seriously believe in the existence of a disembodied *Über-mensch* who had supposedly once turned himself into a Jewish carpenter's son? (I would say the same today.) Whenever a Russian asked me if I believed in *Bog* (and in Soviet times, almost everyone I met in Russia claimed to be a believer), I preferred to say no. '*Dieu*' was also a problem, being such a masculine sort of noun. 'God', on the other hand, was something whose existence I had always been prepared to entertain. Unlike the dreadful Byzantine *Bogi* glaring down at me from numerous cupolas, 'God' (thank goodness I spoke English) didn't even have to be a person or a thing. There was something excitingly centrifugal about 'God'. 'God' had possibilities. Turgenev, however, in dismissing *Bog* as of no more interest than Chinese chequers, resigned himself to the notion that the universe was everything. He seemed annoyingly uninterested in any other kind of spiritual thinking.

Mostly, however, I didn't take his anguish seriously because I failed to see that at the heart of his despair and dread lay a simple, astoundingly modern perception: human life is a hopeless battle with time; and, unless love is possible, that's *all* it is; and love is hardly possible any more. (So naturally Sanin's mind flew to a remembrance of it.)

———

Love hardly possible? It seemed absurd – so absurd that I made a *pppfh* sound, sitting on my bench, and laughed out loud. (A schoolboy passing by whispered to his friend: 'Must be a Pole.' But I heard. I paid no attention.) Absurd because the whole world is awash with love. Every song on the radio, every television drama, every movie we see is about love. Octavio Paz goes further: 'the history of European and American literatures,' he claims, 'is the history of the metamorphoses of love.' In some moods could not I myself interpret everything I did – every cup of tea I made, every sock I washed, my very presence here at Spasskoye – as a detail in a gigantic painting (an amateurish affair, but all my own work) called 'Love'? For my partner in life, my friends, language, literature, the world around me.

Indeed, what about Turgenev himself? This was the man who deeply loved one woman all his life (and several others in little surges). Was that an illusion? Sitting at those desks in Paris, Bougival and the house behind me, he wrote about almost nothing else. Yes, the love affairs in his stories all ended badly – one of the lovers always ran away, died or turned out to be married – but that didn't mean, surely, that nobody had loved. Had Lavretsky not loved Liza and she him? Or Litvinov the perfidious Irina? Had not almost everyone loved Nezhdanov, at least at first? All the other things in his books – the political discussions, the arguments about the fate of Russia, the skirmishes between conservatives and radicals, Slavophiles and Westernisers – are really just the 'age and body of the time' (in Hamlet's words) in which amorous passions are played out.

———

Right here beside this pond, for that matter, a love scene from Turgenev's last passion had been played out. It happened in July 1881, just over two years before he died. Perhaps 'passion' is not quite the right word, but, as is so often the case with Turgenev, it's extraordinarily difficult in our matter-of-fact times to come up with the right word for what he experienced.

I'D ACTUALLY BEEN REMINDED of this last *amour* of his – both bliss-ful and hopeless, as one of his biographers calls it, quoting the poet Tyutchev – while driving through Mtsensk on our way to Spasskoye that very morning. It was at Mtsensk railway station, of all places – a grand red and white building, desolate but florid, still standing in a sea of mud puddles at the end of a street of low, wooden cottages – that the affair reached its strange, touching climax. (It was at Mtsensk rail-way station, too, that Chekhov once drank a cup of coffee he said tasted of smoked fish.) If it weren't for this climax, I doubt that any-body today would remember Maria Savina, and the tender flame she lit in the great man's soul not long before he died.

The flame may have been tender, and may have flickered out quite quickly – at any rate, well before his soul did – but, in typical fashion, when it first sprang up, it put his political enthusiasms of the spring of 1879 firmly in the shade. As in his art, so in his life.

On a visit home from France, he had just been accorded an un-expectedly rapturous welcome by audiences at Moscow and St

Petersburg Universities. In Moscow such was the frenzy to pay homage to this last of the 'men of the forties', the generation of Bakunin and Belinsky, that a police colonel had had to escort him from the hall. His hotels in both cities were in constant uproar as throngs of admirers sought to speak with him. Little wonder that for a few mad weeks, he was tempted to imagine that he was indeed 'interested in politics' and could play some real part in the political transformation of Russia.

In February and March that year, during his visit, the country was a powder-keg. At the same time as acts of terror and other 'distressing manifestations' of extremism, as Turgenev called them, were on the rise, with revolutionaries spilling out onto the streets in violent demonstrations, a constitution allowing for limited representative government was also in the wind and large numbers of students were choosing to agitate for change peacefully. Turgenev, who had abhorred revolutionary violence all his life, even in Paris in 1848, found himself riding high on the new wave.

He understood perfectly well that the standing ovations and student deputations did not mean respect for his art. 'Young people are charged with electricity like a Leyden jar,' he said, 'and I play the part of the device which discharges it.'

Still, these were heady days for the exile whose homeland had reacted to his last novel – indeed to his last four novels – with unremitting hostility. Just two years earlier (aged fifty-nine), in his flat in the rue de Douai, he'd noted in his diary: 'I am once again sitting at my desk. Downstairs my poor friend is singing something in her completely cracked voice. Deep inside me it's darker than the dark of night. It is as if the grave were hastening to swallow me up. The day flies past like a moment – empty, purposeless, colourless. Before you know it, it's time to fall into bed. I have neither the right nor the desire to live; there's nothing more to do, nothing to expect, nothing even to wish for . . .' Well, now there was: the cloud-cuckoo land of a civilised Russia, with himself as one of its leading lights.

———

And so, in the midst of all this brouhaha, he stumbled on a second, even stronger reason to stay alive: he met Maria Savina. A vivacious young actress with bohemian habits, Savina was playing the part of Vera in the almost miraculous revival of his theatrical flop of 1872, *A Month in the Country*. His fantasies of taking a leading, dignified role in reforming Russia were elbowed aside. He was in love again. At sixty. It was the free and forceful married woman up there in front of the footlights all over again. And again, although she was only twenty-five, she was by no means beautiful: indeed, although he found her features 'pretty', if 'sour', he thought her voice 'frightful', like 'a big-nosed Russian servant girl's'.

Even a year later, for the unveiling of the Pushkin monument in Moscow, he was so preoccupied with working out how to meet Savina at Mtsensk railway station that he couldn't be bothered writing more than a mediocre speech. The triumphant performance that day was his old adversary's, Dostoyevsky's. When Dostoyevsky came to the end of his speech, to tumultuous applause, even Turgenev blew him a kiss.

His arrival at Mtsensk railway station that May evening in 1880 was a disarmingly foolish, romantic gesture. After a year of *rendez-vous*, visits to the theatre to see her perform and letter-writing (with all the hand-kissing and ambiguous flattery that infatuations brought out in him), Savina had told him that on 28 May she would be taking the train from Moscow to Odessa. It would stop briefly in Mtsensk, not twenty kilometres from his estate. In a flurry of excitement, Turgenev worked out that he could join her in her compartment for the short stretch to Oryol. Just one hour. He couldn't resist.

All we really know about that hour in the train is that they kissed. 'If I live for a hundred years I shall never forget those kisses,' he wrote to her the following year. And since Turgenev refers to a 'bolt' closing a door of some kind during the journey, we can surmise as well that Savina also said no to something, but to what, we have no idea – possibly to getting off the train in Oryol and spending the night with him there in a hotel. However, the suggestion that she said no to a quick coupling between stops strikes me as preposterous.

Knowing nothing has not stopped any number of biographers and commentators – even the English writer Julian Barnes – from coming up with endless speculations, including the quick coupling possibility. A century or more after this journey took place, we imagine everything from heavy petting (with Turgenev, it is sometimes hinted, unable to achieve an erection) to a formal proposal of marriage (Savina being at this point between husbands). When we read lines such as the following, in a letter he wrote to her after he'd left the train to spend a melancholy night alone in an Oryol hotel, we can come to only one conclusion: 'If the bolt must remain closed, you had better not write to me . . . but I kiss your hands, your feet, and everything you'll allow me to kiss . . . and even what you will not allow.' The conclusion we can't avoid is that Turgenev made a fool of himself in the train, the kind of fool all men make of themselves at eighteen or twenty – or used to, I have no idea whether or not things have changed as much as they appear to have done.

Most commentators seem to view this train journey as a titillating, slightly pathetic, but endearingly romantic last throw on Turgenev's part. He himself called it his 'last flaring of the lamp', using a word most often used of the little lamp set before an icon. I can't see what the mystery is. Or why it is either titillating or pathetic.

Whether Turgenev and Savina confined themselves to kissing each other on the lips or he sought to kiss her where she would not allow it strikes me as of no consequence. Whether or not after their embrace he begged her to leap out into the night with him at Oryol and hurry off to a hotel seems to me beside the point – if the point is to understand Turgenev's attitude to love.

Nothing could be more normal, I'd have thought, than that a man who has loved one woman for thirty-five years (and Pauline was now the pivot of his very being, not some love object) should from time to time find himself struck by the urgent desire for intimacy with somebody else. 'Intimacy' is, I think, the key word. It's not as commonly used in Russian as it is in English – and certainly Turgenev, when he wrote to Savina after this mad-cap adventure, spoke not of intimacy, but of his 'insurmountable longing to merge, to possess and to surrender myself'. (Shades of Lavretsky over twenty years earlier.) But what is intimacy if not precisely this double-sided vulnerability? Possession *and* surrender, and therefore fusion.

To us the word 'intimacy' has strong sexual overtones – as did 'possession' and 'surrender', for that matter, for Turgenev. Obviously, for good biological reasons, a twenty-year-old youth will dream of intimacy in more pressingly sexual terms than a sixty-year-old, in particular the singular intimacy that comes with knowing somebody at the indescribable moment of orgasm. Later in life, however, most of us dream of something more all-encompassing than this. We still dream of knowing somebody utterly – of touching somebody beautiful and being touched (and for many at sixty touching is a painfully rare pleasure), of gently laying ourselves bare and at the same time exploring whatever corner we wish of this being we find so beautiful, but what we hunger for is so much wider, or perhaps deeper, than copulation that we find ourselves able to take delight in an intimacy for which the thought of copulation is just a background melody.

Like Turgenev, alone again, one might well feel 'deeply sorry that this lovely night has been lost forever without touching me with its wing'. Nonetheless, part of us also knows that we've escaped humiliation and boredom by the skin of our teeth.

———

The paradox which many in conventional arrangements have difficulty understanding is that what made this infatuation with Savina possible, and so rewarding, was precisely the fact that Turgenev loved Pauline Viardot. If he had not loved her as he did, if hers had not been the very face of love for him, if he had not been securely and forever anchored to her, then this episode with a distinctly unanchored bohemian could not have taken place. Or it would have turned into something else, something either dangerous or pathetic. It was mad and delicious *because* he loved Viardot.

As for the troubadour, this courtship was possible for Turgenev, a joy and without consequence, *because* it was in some sense adulterous. An airy triangle was attractive to Ivan Sergeyevich in his mature years *because* the base line was so firm. (It was, after all, the hypotenuse of another utterly stable triangle which had Louis Viardot at its apex.) No wonder he could preface his remarks about an 'insurmountable longing to merge' with a question to himself: 'Am I in love with you? I don't know.'

Only in the sloppiest sense of the word did he even 'love [her] very much', as he claimed the following year. (In Russian this exasperating verb is used with even greater abandon than in English. Russians 'love' – *lyubyat* – just about anything and anyone they feel a rush of affection for, or even just quite like.) In fact, just a couple of months after the incident in the train, when they both happened to be in Paris, Savina didn't even tell Turgenev she was there – and he was not put out. 'She has ceased to exist for me,' he told a friend of his. They did eventually meet again, but it was not an intimate *rendez-vous*.

The following year he remembered the treasured kisses in the train, as one does, and allowed himself to rekindle the guttering flame. ('I love you very much – much more than I should, but that is not my fault.' This sounds like a line from a popular French novel.) At the same time he was writing to Pauline's daughter, Claudie, in Bougival: 'You speak to me of Mlle Savina! She has reappeared for a moment and is now disappearing again. My thermometer as far as she is concerned has dropped back below "warm". Her fish mouth, her vulgar nose and her coarse voice make me forget her eyes, which are beautiful and full of life, but not kind.' With a desperate final flourish, he adds in German: 'She is forgotten and never to be brought to mind!'

Needless to say, she was not forgotten at all. Even Claudie, on guard, no doubt, against interlopers, must have seen through the ruse. Why would he have forgotten her? One might mentally mislay a marriage or two, but not an infatuation – at least, in my experience. One rehearses infatuations forever. As Oscar Wilde put it, exaggerating as usual: 'The only difference between a caprice and a life-long passion is that the caprice lasts a little longer.'

In July 1881, far from forgotten, Savina did something that Pauline Viardot in forty years never found the time to do, although Turgenev planned for it and fantasised about it all his life: she came to Spasskoye. The five days and nights of high-spirited fun – singing around the piano, drinking champagne with visiting friends, watching the peasants sing and dance in the park – led and could lead nowhere: she was about to marry again (disastrously, as it happens) and he was wedded for all eternity to Pauline Viardot. That's why she could come to Spasskoye. That's why they could play at being lovers – stroll in the park in the evening exchanging the occasional kiss, for instance, or sit in her room together ('Savina's room' is still there, as chaste as a nun's cell) while he read her moving passages from his *Poems in Prose* or his dazzlingly erotic story 'Song of Triumphant Love'.

And that is also why, one warm afternoon that July, beside this very pond I was sitting gazing at, he had waited hoping for a glimpse of Savina in her bathing costume while she splashed about in the enclosure he'd had built to safeguard her modesty. In the event, to Turgenev's chagrin, it was his friend Polonsky who was vouchsafed a flash of white flesh as Savina left the water, but perhaps that just made the escapade more piquant.

Certainly when he got back to Bougival three months later Turgenev's imagination was sufficiently stimulated to write to her provocatively, picturing the two of them visiting Venice together. They take a ride in a gondola, they look at paintings, they have dinner together and then, after spending the evening at the theatre . . . 'my imagination stops respectfully'. It's a common enough fantasy, even if most of us don't quite get around to writing it down, putting a stamp on the envelope and posting it. Just the two of us, outside time, with no ties to our everyday lives, somewhere beautiful where we know nobody and there will be no consequences. A snapshot of paradise. For me it's usually a tango palace in Buenos Aires, it's after midnight, and then . . . (There my imagination grows misty – but probably, as Turgenev hinted in his letter to Savina, less because there is something to keep hidden than because there would be nothing to hide.) For others the 'what if' might unfold in Fez or Kathmandu. It is the 'what-ifness' that makes you want to try out hundreds of endings in your mind, sometimes over decades. A time comes when 'what if' is just about all you have to keep expectation alive. It's not a tragedy, and it's not a farce, it's romance.

———

By the following year, when they met again in Paris, the infatuation had run its course – which is what infatuations do, that is their whole point and their delight. All the same, at Turgenev's memorial service in St Petersburg a year later, Maria Savina joined other celebrities in reading from his works. She chose 'Faust', a supernatural story of forbidden love ending in death. Had there been a touch more, then, to this fleeting affair than a few stolen kisses in the half-dark? Given the audience, her appearance at the service was more probably simply a smart career move.

AT THE FAR END OF THE POND a sudden breeze had begun dancing on the water, pitting its grey surface with splashes of greenish light. Behind me, amongst the trees in the park, I could hear the squawks of more schoolchildren approaching. What on earth could they be making of Spasskoye?

Somewhere near the gates to the estate Kolya would be waiting for me with the car. I should really be getting back. Taking a roundabout track to avoid the children, I plunged into the gloom of the park and headed for the house.

So what could it mean to say, as I'd thought to myself just before I'd said *pppfh* and been called a Pole, that love was hardly possible any more, especially for a man like Turgenev? And, even if it were true, why should it follow that each human life was therefore nothing but a hopeless battle with time? What difference could love make?

Lust was obviously not impossible for Turgenev – after all, he'd produced a daughter, so profoundly uninteresting that it's difficult to think of a thing to say about her except that she was unwisely called Paulinette, became a Frenchwoman and even contrived to forget her native language. And, in a letter to a male friend at the age of forty-one he said quite clearly that he enjoyed sex four times a year – but that was enough. Lust is obviously not impossible nowadays, either. Where I come from it's an inalienable right, lustfulness being a measure of one's worth as a well-rounded human being.

Nor was sentimental attachment, lust's chaperone, impossible for Turgenev's generation any more than it is for us. Or falling *in* love. Or deep affection, passion, adoration, married bliss, abiding fondness or any number of other things that go under the general heading of 'love'. All his life Turgenev had romantic attachments, flings, passionate *amours*, passing infatuations – and wrote about them constantly, as we do today. So what was 'hardly possible' about love?

By the late nineteenth century what was hardly possible for an educated freethinker to believe in was the kind of love that ruptures time. And nowadays, except at the height of lovesickness, with music in the background (both Mahler and Piaf are perfect), it's virtually impossible: erotically liberated, we have lost sight of love altogether. It is still possible to believe that desire could split you in half like lightning or that affection could carry you comfortably through the years like a gently rocking boat; it is still possible to believe you might go mad with unrequited lust or feel symphonically amplified by spending the night with this one or that; in fact, whole sectors of the economy, even in Russia nowadays, are devoted to making sure you believe these kinds of love can still flower and know where to buy the products you'll need to make them germinate. For none of these loves, however, do you need a soul. These are all mortal loves. You can love in all these ways without actually existing, except as a doomed tangle of neurones and synapses with a mouth that says 'I'. You can love in all these ways and still believe that the universe is all there is.

The love that saves us from time (and therefore queues – indeed, linearity of every kind), or at least opens up a crack in it, allowing us, in Octavio Paz's phrase, to 'think we have glimpsed the other side', is of a different order. It is this kind of love which seemed hardly possible any more to the mature Turgenev. If it proved impossible, that would mean that what we see is all there is. And that would mean that ultimately everything is futile.

Hardly possible, but worth hoping for.

According to one of his most understanding biographers, Boris Zaitsev, Turgenev could not abide the crudities his friends indulged in over their dinners in Parisian restaurants when they touched (as they often did) on the subject of *l'amour*. A gourmet himself when it came to food, Zaitsev writes, Turgenev could not abide his companions' gastronomic approach to love. He was still convinced, however irrational it might seem, that love could be 'a mystical shaft of light' – and here Zaitsev uses a revealing word, *prosvet,* which means both a shaft of light piercing the darkness (and so a ray of hope) and an opening in a wall which lets light into a gloomy interior. Inviting the ridicule of his worldly companions, Turgenev even asserted that in the eyes of a beloved woman you could discern 'divinity' – Being, in other words, outside time, although perceived from within it. It's not hard to imagine how that sort of thing went down with Zola and company. When he got home to the rue de Douai he may well have felt a little awkward about it himself. In whose eyes had he ever seen timeless Being?

———

Like a playful sign from the gods, shafts of pale light were beginning to break through the gloom in the wood as I walked back towards the house. The mauve-green mistiness was lifting. Up ahead I could see Kolya sitting peaceably on the steps of the front veranda in a patch of soft sunlight. 'You're a writer,' he'd said to me when I set off by myself to find the pond, 'a *creative* person, so you need to be alone to think.' Well, I hadn't quite finished thinking yet, so I veered off behind the house towards the old stables. I needed a few more minutes alone to come up with my own words to help me nut out the love which it is virtually impossible to believe in any more.

'The sweep of being' came to mind. Not having Zola and Flaubert with me to snort derisively, just rooks, I didn't feel awkward at all about murmuring this phrase to myself. It's the sweep of being we believe we've glimpsed – instantaneously – when we're seized by the love that saves us from time. All of a sudden, for no reason at all, without our willing it, we are flying towards that opening in the wall of time, becoming at one with the sweep of being beyond it. In that first instant we do something impossible: we recognise the unknown. It does happen – rarely, in reality almost never, but it does happen.

It even happens to dyed-in-the-wool rationalists such as Turgenev's own Bazarov in *Fathers and Sons,* the man who has declared love to be an 'unpardonable imbecility'. All those Minnesingers and troubadours, in his opinion, rabbiting on about snowy breasts and dying of longing, should have been clapped in a lunatic asylum. When it happens to him he is so shaken that he actually commits suicide – or at least dies after showing a wilful disregard for his own life.

A century and a half later, if we suspect it's happening to us, we might murmur 'I'll love you forever' and hum along for a while to songs about 'loving you until the end of time', but in our hearts we don't believe it. Words like 'I' and 'you' just don't mean what they once did. Our word-bound imagination failing us, we settle for lust mixed with sentimental attachment. And – the last throw of the dice in the losing game with time – children.

Only religion, as Turgenev noted ruefully, has made any serious attempt to call time's bluff and remove our fear of the executioner. Yet, for all its huffing and puffing, what a huge disappointment Western religion has turned out to be. We were expecting so much more. The music, paintings and cathedrals don't make up for it. Jesus mentioned something about the kingdom of God being revealed to us – and quickly, too – and what might that be, if not a rent in the fabric of time? However, as Mark Twain remarked, what we got instead, with lightning speed, was the Church.

In Turgenev's experience (although not in mine, I must admit), religion simply threw up more mysteries and, as we know, he could not bring himself to believe in mysteries. Although Romantically inclined, he was still the child of the Enlightenment. The natural universe is a sphinx, he wrote in his mid-forties to a friend of his, which has 'looked at me with its huge motionless eyes, all the more terrible for not seeking to arouse fear. Not knowing the key to the riddle is cruel, but it is perhaps even crueller to have to tell yourself that there is no key because there is no longer any riddle. Flies knocking without respite against a pane of glass – that, I think, is the perfect symbol of who we are.'

ON OUR WAY BACK TO THE CAR, right by Spasskoye's main gates, I stopped to look at the church Turgenev had had built for his peasants with typical generosity of spirit. Whatever his own views on religion were, he knew that for most of his peasants the Orthodox service was the only truly beautiful thing in their lives, the only hint of the unearthly. Borne aloft on the sound of the bells and the singing, dazzled by the vestments, candles, frescoes and gilded iconostasis, breathing in the incense-laden air, they could almost believe in the miracle of transcendence.

'Do you want to go in?' I asked Kolya. The building was being extensively restored, but the door was open and there were lights burning inside.

'No, but you go,' he said. 'I'll see you back at the car.'

Now that churches are no longer a forbidden zone, it's remarkable how indifferent most Russians seem to be to them. This was unexpected. A century ago most Russians would probably have thought of themselves as Orthodox, believers in the True Glory, rather than

Russian. In the sixties and seventies when I was a student in Moscow, all sorts of people who in the West would not have darkened the doors of a church between their christening and their funeral would confess to religious longings, collect icons, wear a cross under their shirt or blouse and speak with glee of secret baptisms and having furtively attended services. Now that the ban on church attendance has been lifted, if the statistics in *Time* magazine are to be believed, fewer Russians than anyone else in Europe, even the Swedes and Danes, bother to go to church with any regularity.

Inside the empty church I was disconcerted to find a stall set up selling religious tracts – booklets explaining why the Russian Orthodox Church was right and everybody else was wrong, pamphlets for children, the lives of the saints, Bibles and so on. It seemed completely out of place at the entrance to a museum devoted to recapturing the life of Turgenev – not the restored church, but the stall peddling modern Orthodoxy. Feeling almost offended on his behalf, I didn't linger.

———

'So have you had a think?' Kolya asked me with a smile as I approached the car. 'Has it been worth the trip?'

'Oh, yes,' I said, 'it's been . . . fantastic.' And in a sense it had been, almost literally. I'd recaptured something, I'd felt like a living bridge across the chasm of time.

The question of what can be recaptured in a museum like Spasskoye is, of course, a complicated one. At some level the whole project of trying to recapture something that was never a *thing* in the first place is doomed to failure. 'Turgenev' was an experience, not a thing, and if you tried to pin it down, turning it into a collection of objects, it would stop being 'Turgenev'.

All the same, in Spasskoye I'd caught up with myself at last, at least as far as Turgenev was concerned.

At that moment, as we chugged out of the carpark, I'd have loved to talk to somebody about what I'd just recaptured, but Kolya was not the right person. It's not that he wouldn't have been interested, but it would have been hard for us to find a common language. The previous evening in the hotel buffet, for instance, during a commercial break on *The Weakest Link*, Kolya had asked me if Turgenev had been married.

'No, he never married,' I said, toying with a rather stale fish sandwich. The buffet had a bit of catching up to do of its own.

'So did he have lovers? This Frenchwoman, Pauline . . .'

'Viardot. Yes. Well, they weren't exactly lovers.'

'You mean they were just friends?'

'No, not exactly just friends either. I don't know the right word. They were like lovers, except that there was no sex. None that we know of, anyway.'

Kolya considered the mayhem unfolding on the screen in the corner while he finished his Fanta. He clearly wanted to know more, but wasn't sure how to put it.

'You see, basically,' I said, choosing my words carefully, 'Turgenev wasn't all that interested in sex. As such.'

'You mean he was impotent?' He, too, was choosing his words carefully – his word for 'impotent' was almost stylish.

'No, not at all,' I said. It was on the tip of my tongue to tell him that for Turgenev four times a year was plenty, but I was unsure about where that might lead us. Our conversation about the 'working girls' beside the highway on the way down from Moscow left me in no doubt that Kolya would find such austerity very odd indeed. 'No, you see, it's just that for him love really didn't work unless it was for a married woman, or at least for a woman who was devoted to somebody else. So sex wasn't out of the question, but it was never going to be what made him love her. For him, you see, Pauline was . . .' And here words failed me. I couldn't bring myself there in that buffet, surrounded by German truck-drivers slurping beetroot soup, to say to a man I hardly knew: 'For him, you see, Pauline was a breach – a *prosvet* – in the wall of time.'

Kolya wasn't pushing me to say more, but I could see that he wasn't following the savagery on the television in the corner with any interest. 'Everyone's very different, that's all,' I said, taking the cowardly way out, 'despite what it might say in *Men's Health*.' He sipped his Fanta thoughtfully, but didn't comment. He probably couldn't afford *Men's Health*, although posters for it featuring the usual honed torsos were all over Moscow. 'Gogol, for example, died a virgin.'

'Well, Tolstoy certainly didn't,' he said. Later, in the Park of Culture and Rest, I had the feeling he was on the verge of asking me what my own arrangement was, but he probably suspected it would turn out to be too 'different' for comfort. We bought ice-creams instead and sat commenting on the passing parade.

ON THE DRIVE BACK TO ORYOL from Spasskoye, passing yet another silent, rusting factory outside Mtsensk, I asked Kolya who he blamed for the devastation we could see all around us – the dilapidated apartment blocks, the hovels huddled on the edge of town, the broken-down buses, the pot-holed roads, the empty shops, the unsmiling crowds. I thought he might say corrupt officials, the Communist Party, or the new market economy, even German capitalists. But all he said was: 'Ilyich.'

'Do you think things will get better one day soon?' I asked after a little pause.

'No.'

'And how does that make you feel?'

'*Vozmushchayus*,' he said. 'Indignant' doesn't quite cover it.

Once upon a time, not so far from Mtsensk, I had seen much the same sort of blighted landscape that now filled Kolya with despair, but I'd been prepared in those days to believe that it would all soon be swept away. It was in October 1966 and I was on an excursion to

Tolstoy's estate at Yasnaya Polyana with a group of other foreign students, my first trip outside the capital. (In those days we couldn't go beyond the city boundaries without a visa. We did, some of us, just for a lark, but it didn't do to get caught.) The trip was 'rather fun', I wrote to my father with my usual relentless brightness when I got back to Moscow that evening, although 'the landscape is not very interesting, really, just rolling hills and paddocks, with towns here and there.' Well, we had rolling hills and paddocks at home. 'Russian towns,' I went on, 'are rather depressing: they consist either of a string of tumble-down wooden houses with weed-filled gardens along the side of the road, with only one or two shops set back from the road fronting onto a dusty, puddle-covered square, or else they are great rambling conglomerations of very grimy, almost ramshackle brick houses, stretching out for miles and miles, with acres and acres of multistoreyed blocks of flats, all identical and set in fields and patches of mud, on the outskirts.' This was not like home.

After nearly forty years it's still a fairly accurate description of many towns I saw on the way back to Oryol with Kolya. God alone knows what they must be like in the backblocks of Siberia. In some hazy sort of way I suppose I'd thought, for no very good reason, that it would now all look much more like Finland.

Driving through the silent, empty countryside south of Mtsensk – all the farm equipment in these parts had broken down, according to Kolya – we hardly spoke. My mind lurched forward to Moscow, where I meant to spend a few more days before leaving for home. I needed to catch up with myself there as well, before going back to the other side of the world. All I'd really felt as Moscow's neon signs, sleek German cars and gleaming new apartment blocks flashed by had been a kind of embarrassed emptiness, the sort of feeling you have sometimes when after many years you meet up again with somebody you were once in love with and find that with the best will in the world you can't recapture what it was that you once found so enchanting. As in Turgenev's study, rather than excited, what I'd mostly felt was askew. Touching down at Moscow airport in 1966 at the age of twenty-two, on the other hand, had been the most thrilling moment in my life.

BACK IN MOSCOW – perhaps because it was a Sunday afternoon – I found that my mood was beginning to change. Besides, the whole city seems to break out in a smile on a springlike Sunday afternoon. I strolled about the old city with friends, taking pleasure in the handsome architecture, the garish churches, even the beautiful wrought-iron fences bordering so many gardens and parks. My mind drifted to the treasure-houses of the Pushkin Museum and the Kremlin, the feasts on offer in the concert-halls and theatres. Who was I, when it all boiled down, to sit in stony-faced judgement on a civilisation as rich as this one? I would end up drowning in clichés. All civilisations, after all, are founded on some notion of barely human hordes on the one hand and the enlightened on the other – 'us'. How we police the border between the civilised and the barbarians may differ, but we all police it, from Togo to Tasmania. What has distinguished Russian civilisation, as Belinsky pointed out, is the colossal inhumanity with which it has policed this border. Nowadays in the

West we try to do it humanely, but it wasn't always so by any means and frequently still isn't.

———

Oddly enough, on that last Sunday afternoon walk with friends around the elegant Prechistenka district, we ran across a small, blue-grey, wooden house with six white columns and a rather scruffy garden out the back. On the wall was a plaque which read (the vague wording was oddly familiar):

> **On a number of occasions**
> **the great Russian writer**
> **Ivan Sergeyevich Turgenev**
> **stayed**
> **in this house**

I recognised it immediately: it was the house his mother had rented in Moscow. They'd had a dacha outside Moscow as well, but he'd often stayed with her here in the 1840s, on his way to St Petersburg or Spasskoye, before he went to France in Pauline's wake.

What was odd was that it was just around the corner from the old Australian Embassy in Kropotkinsky Pereulok. I used to drop in to the Embassy once or twice a week during my student days, mostly to pick up mail, so I must have passed the Turgenevs' house dozens of times without noticing. I failed to notice many things, I now realise. On reflection, I think I was basically on safari in Russia during my student years, like so many Westerners – for that matter, like so many Westerners visiting my own country. I only had eyes for the object of my quest. For example, I failed to notice that the Australian Embassy was one of Fyodor Shekhtel's Art Nouveau masterpieces, built for a textile baron's mistress in 1901. Making my way into the grounds past the dour-faced guard, I remember, I used to find its severely geometrical, tiled exterior, with the enormous windows at the front flooding the panelled interior with light, remarkably ugly.

Unlike Tolstoy's house in a nearby street, the Turgenevs' house is all shut up and obviously has not become a place of pilgrimage. Inside, I understand, they've uncovered the original wallpaper from 1827. I'd have liked to see it, I'd have liked to see what colour it is, the light in the rooms, the proportions, the long-gone old furniture. Then, as at Spasskoye or Bougival, I might have been able to catch some echo of Turgenev's real voice. In the end that's why I was there. Reading Turgenev – or Tolstoy or Gogol or Dostoyevsky, anyone from a time and place we can barely imagine any more – is a disembodied experience unless we know what it felt like to be alive there then. The simplest sentence – 'Marfa Timofeyevna came downstairs when the soup was already on the table' – is just a blur, a succession of ordinary English words, unless we can hear a real voice speaking them. I mean that we must feel that the voice comes from a real throat, beneath real eyes, ears, nose and even tongue (since there's soup on the table), that the owner of the voice once really lived and (mysteriously) even suspected our presence there, listening. Then all those clusters of colourless syllables – 'Marfa Timofeyevna', 'downstairs', 'soup', 'table' – will detonate softly, filling our mind with the sound of creaking wood, the colour of the table-cloth and the mahogany table-legs beneath it, the smell of the soup in its porcelain bowl. We'll see Marfa Timofeyevna holding with one hand the ends of her (unmentioned) knitted shawl across her bosom, the (unmentioned) serving maid standing over by the wall (covered in wallpaper in a striking neo-classical pattern), we'll see the shadows the lamplight casts and how kind it is to Marfa Timofeyevna's complexion, we'll feel the warmth from the tiled oven in the corner . . . we'll be there, in a word. And the speaker will know we're there. And the complicity will be delicious.

Staring at the plaque on the wall of the house at Ostozhenka 37 would evoke none of this. When Turgenev and his mother stayed here in the 1840s, the house would have been close to the outskirts of the city, while now it's surrounded by palaces and elegant nineteenth-century merchants' mansions all being busily restored as luxury apartment blocks for foreigners and the seriously wealthy. Across the road from the house is a smart, new restaurant with an English name, and there's a charming Italian eating-house just round the corner near the old embassy. The Ivan Sergeyevich Turgenev who lived in this house, drank tea in this garden, heard the bells of Moscow's churches booming all day long, and set off in his carriage up the street I was standing in to go to the theatre or visit friends remains disembodied.

It was while he was coming and going from this house, of course, that the idea was forming in his mind of leaving Russia for the civilised West. What he, the most civilised of men, may have been seeking, I now tend to think, was not so much escape from barbarism, as escape from the civilisation of 'Seville' – not that 'Seville' would have meant to him then what it means to me now: he first left Russia nearly half a century before Dostoyevsky wrote *The Brothers Karamazov*.

Turgenev had no need of Dostoyevsky, however, to understand the ideas Russian civilisation was founded on – not that Dostoyevsky would have agreed that Orthodox Russia under Nicholas I was 'Seville' at all, he was writing a warning, not a commentary. At an early age, like so many of his generation (the 'men of the forties' – Belinsky,

Annenkov, Nekrasov, Fet, Bakunin, Herzen), Turgenev refused to believe that society must choose between bread and freedom. An aristocrat in every fibre of his being, he saw no reason to believe that the hordes were by nature slaves to be lulled by mysteries and lashed into submission in order to be fed. In Germany and France Turgenev believed he'd find a different, more humane, balance between bread and freedom. And in Pauline Viardot, so dazzlingly free, in her castle at Courtavenel, he no doubt believed as an enlightened aristocrat that he'd found the very embodiment of the superior civilisation he'd been seeking and he gave her his heart.

'So you enjoyed yourself yesterday,' Irina said to me the next morning when we met to say goodbye. 'I'm glad. Who knows, one day you might even come to like Moscow after all.'

'I feel reconciled to Moscow,' I said, thinking of what Tolstoy had written after visiting Turgenev at Spasskoye: 'His house showed me his roots . . . it reconciled me to him.' The Russian word he chose is a beautiful one – *primiril*. Spasskoye *primiril* him to his old friend and antagonist. It means 'brought us together and gave us peace'.

As it happens, this was one of Turgenev's favourite words. He lived by it. Human life may seem pointless and always end badly, but you must make your peace with it. If lasting happiness escapes you, you must resign yourself to magnifying the blissful moments. If burning passion kaleidoscopes into something slower, mellower and more sweet-tempered, then you must have the grace to warm yourself by this gentler flame. If shafts of light are rare, or only a mirage, wait for them quietly all the same. If love, when you try to lay hold of it with your hands or even just your heart, slips from your grasp like water because there's no one there, you must reconcile yourself to loving what you find. Love is never enough. It must always be enough. There's nothing else. That, at least, is what I hear him say when he talks to me.

Home again, I'm warming to the idea of rereading Turgenev.

CHRONOLOGY

TURGENEV		MEANWHILE	
		1809:	GOGOL BORN
1818:	BORN IN ORYOL, SOUTHERN RUSSIA; BROUGHT UP AT NEARBY SPASSKOYE		
		1821:	DOSTOYEVSKY BORN; PAULINE VIARDOT BORN
		1825:	ALEXANDER I DIES; NICHOLAS I ON THRONE
		1828:	TOLSTOY BORN
1833:	ENTERS MOSCOW UNIVERSITY		
1834:	ENTERS ST PETERSBURG UNIVERSITY; FATHER DIES	*1837*:	PUSHKIN DIES
1838:	ENTERS BERLIN UNIVERSITY		
1839:	SPASSKOYE LARGELY DESTROYED BY FIRE	*1840*:	PAULINE MARRIES LOUIS VIARDOT (B. 1800)
1841:	RETURNS TO RUSSIA FROM GERMANY		
1842:	DAUGHTER PAULINETTE BORN	*1842*:	*DEAD SOULS* PUB. (GOGOL)
1843:	MEETS PAULINE AND LOUIS VIARDOT		
1845:	FIRST SHORT VISIT TO COURTAVENEL WHILE TOURING EUROPE		

CHRONOLOGY

TURGENEV		MEANWHILE	
1847:	RETURNS TO FRANCE AND COURTAVENEL; BEGINS WRITING *A HUNTER'S NOTES*	*1847*:	BELINSKY'S LETTER TO GOGOL
		1848:	REVOLUTION IN PARIS; SECOND REPUBLIC DECLARED UNDER LOUIS NAPOLEON
		1849:	DOSTOYEVSKY SENT TO SIBERIA FOR NINE YEARS
1850:	WRITES *A MONTH IN THE COUNTRY*; RETURNS TO SPASSKOYE; MOTHER DIES		
1852:	EXILED TO SPASSKOYE	*1852*:	GOGOL DIES; LOUIS NAPOLEON DECLARES HIMSELF EMPEROR
1853:	ILLEGAL MEETING WITH PAULINE IN MOSCOW	*1853*:	CRIMEAN WAR BEGINS
		1855:	NICHOLAS I DIES; ALEXANDER II ON THRONE
1856:	PUBLISHES FIRST NOVEL, *RUDIN*; SHORT VISIT TO COURTAVENEL	*1856*:	CRIMEAN WAR ENDS
1858:	AFTER THIS DATE SPENDS MOST OF HIS TIME ABROAD, VISITING RUSSIA OCCASIONALLY		
1859:	REVISITS COURTAVENEL; *NEST OF THE GENTRY* PUB.		
1860:	*ON THE EVE* PUB.		
		1861:	EMANCIPATION OF THE SERFS
1862:	*FATHERS AND SONS* PUB.		
1863:	MOVES TO SCHILLERSTRASSE IN BADEN-BADEN	*1863-9*:	*WAR AND PEACE* PUB.
		1864:	*NOTES FROM UNDERGROUND* PUB. (DOSTOYEVSKY)
		1866:	*CRIME AND PUNISHMENT* PUB.
1867:	*SMOKE* PUB.		

TURGENEV		MEANWHILE	
1868:	MOVES TO VILLA ON FREMERSBERGSTR.	1868:	*THE IDIOT* PUB.
1870:	LEAVES BADEN-BADEN	1870-1:	FRANCO-PRUSSIAN WAR
1871:	SETTLES IN PARIS (RUE DE DOUAI), FREQUENTLY RETURNING TO SPASSKOYE	1871:	*THE POSSESSED* PUB. (DOSTOYEVSKY)
1872:	*TORRENTS OF SPRING* PUB.		
		1875-7:	*ANNA KARENINA* PUB.
1876:	OCCUPIES CHALET AT BOUGIVAL		
1877:	*VIRGIN SOIL* PUB.		
1879:	TRIUMPHANT RETURN TO RUSSIA; MEETS SAVINA		
1880:	MEETS SAVINA IN TRAIN	1880:	*THE BROTHERS KARAMAZOV* PUB.
1881:	SAVINA VISITS SPASSKOYE	1881:	ALEXANDER II ASSASSINATED; ALEXANDER III ON THRONE
1883 (SEPTEMBER):	DIES AT BOUGIVAL	1883 (MAY):	LOUIS VIARDOT DIES
		1894:	ALEXANDER III DIES; NICHOLAS II ON THRONE
1906:	FIRE AT SPASSKOYE	1910:	PAULINE VIARDOT DIES
1976:	SPASSKOYE PARTIALLY REBUILT		

ACKNOWLEDGEMENTS

Following in Turgenev's footsteps was made possible through the kindness and practical assistance of Pierrick Tillet and Nicole Kormendi in France and Glenn and Agnès Waller in Russia. I am deeply grateful to all of them. I would also like to express my sincere thanks to Judith Lukin-Amundsen, my editor, for her discerning comments and sensitive reshaping of my manuscript.

My greatest debt of gratitude in writing this book, however, is to Natalie Staples of Hobart, Tasmania, who not only inspired me to set off on my travels in the first place, but, throughout the writing process, shared with me her deep knowledge of Russian language and culture, plied me with books and articles I would never have unearthed on my own, commented on my manuscript at every stage of the writing and unfailingly offered me the encouragement I needed to complete my task.

She is, of course, in no way responsible for the views and interpretations of Turgenev's works expressed in these pages, but without her there would have been no journey and no book.